CREATIVE Junior High PROGRAMS

From A to Z

VOL. 1 (A-M)

13 complete, ready-to-use topical meetings

YOUTH SPECIALTIES TITLES

Professional Resources
Developing Spiritual Growth in Junior High Students
Developing Student Leaders
Equipped to Serve: Volunteer Youth Worker Training Course
Help! I'm a Sunday School Teacher!
Help! I'm a Volunteer Youth Worker!
How to Expand Your Youth Ministry
How to Recruit and Train Volunteer Youth Workers
The Ministry of Nurture
One Kid at a Time: Reaching Youth Through Mentoring
Peer Counseling in Youth Groups
Advanced Peer Counseling in Youth Groups

Discussion Starter Resources
Get 'Em Talking
4th-6th Grade TalkSheets
High School TalkSheets
Junior High TalkSheets
High School TalkSheets: Psalms and Proverbs
Junior High TalkSheets: Psalms and Proverbs
More High School TalkSheets
More Junior High TalkSheets
Parent Ministry TalkSheets
What If...? Provocative Questions to Get Teenagers Talking, Thinking, Doing
Would You Rather...? 465 Questions to Get Kids Talking

Ideas Library
Combos: 1-4, 5-8, 9-12, 13-16, 17-20, 21-24, 25-28, 29-32, 33-36, 37-40, 41-44, 45-48, 49-52, 53-56
Singles: 53, 54, 55
Ideas Index

Youth Ministry Programming
Compassionate Kids: Practical Ways to Involve Kids in Mission and Service
Creative Bible Lessons in John: Encounters with Jesus
Creative Bible Lessons in Romans: Faith on Fire!
Creative Bible Lessons on the Life of Christ
Creative Junior High Programs from A to Z, Vol. 1 (A-M)
Creative Programming Ideas for Junior High Ministry
Creative Socials and Special Events
Dramatic Pauses

Facing Your Future: Graduating Youth Groups with a Faith that Lasts
Great Fundraising Ideas for Youth Groups
More Great Fundraising Ideas for Youth Groups
Great Retreats for Youth Groups
Greatest Skits on Earth
Greatest Skits on Earth, Vol. 2
Hot Illustrations for Youth Talks
Memory Makers
More Hot Illustrations for Youth Talks
Hot Talks
Incredible Questionnaires for Youth Ministry
Junior High Game Nights
More Junior High Game Nights
Play It! Great Games for Groups
Play It Again! More Great Games for Groups
Road Trip
Spontaneous Melodramas
Super Sketches for Youth Ministry
Teaching the Bible Creatively
Up Close and Personal: How to Build Community in Your Youth Group
Worship Services for Youth Groups

Clip Art
ArtSource Vol. 1—Fantastic Activities
ArtSource Vol. 2—Borders, Symbols, Holidays, and Attention Getters
ArtSource Vol. 3—Sports
ArtSource Vol. 4—Phrases and Verses
ArtSource Vol. 5—Amazing Oddities and Appalling Images
ArtSource Vol. 6—Spiritual Topics
ArtSource Vol. 7—Variety Pack
ArtSource CD-ROM (contains Volumes 1-7)

Videos
Edge TV
God Views
The Heart of Youth Ministry: A Morning with Mike Yaconelli
Next Time I Fall in Love Video Curriculum
Promo Spots for Junior High Game Nights
Understanding Your Teenager Video Curriculum

Student Books
Grow For It Journal
Grow For It Journal through the Scriptures
Wild Truth Journal for Junior Highers
101 Things to Do during a Dull Sermon

CREATIVE Junior High PROGRAMS From A to Z

VOL. 1 (A-M)

13 complete, ready-to-use topical meetings

Steve Dickie & Darrell Pearson

Youth Specialties

ZondervanPublishingHouse

Grand Rapids, Michigan
A Division of HarperCollinsPublishers

Creative Junior High Programs from A to Z, Vol. 1 (A-M): 13 complete, ready-to-use topical meetings
Copyright © 1996 by Youth Specialties, Inc.

Youth Specialties Books, 1224 Greenfield Dr., El Cajon, CA 92021, are published by Zondervan Publishing House, 5300 Patterson S.E., Grand Rapids, MI 49530.

Library of Congress Cataloging-in-Publication Data

Dickie, Steve, 1956-
    Creative junior high programs from A to Z / Steve Dickie & Darrell Pearson
        p. cm.
    Contents: v. 1. A-M — v. 2. N-Z
    ISBN 0-310-20779-7 (v. 1). — ISBN 0-310-21158-1 (v. 2)
    1. Church group work with teenagers. I. Pearson, Darrell, 1954-
        II. Title
BV4447.D479 1996
268'.433—dc20

96-20119
CIP

Edited by Sheri Stanley
Cover and interior design by Patton Brothers Design

Printed in the United States of America

96 97 98 99/ /4 3 2 1

To our parents, Willard and Eileen Pearson and James and Martha Dickie.

Contents

Darrell's acknowledgments

Thank you, Dave VanBenschoten, Vince Beer, and Lindsay Case, for believing in me—with the full knowledge that you'd likely never see that money again. And thanks to Noel Becchetti, Michelle Wilson, and Tim McLaughlin, who showed more grace than was deserved.

Steve's acknowledgements

To the junior high kids and staff at Bel Air Presbyterian Church in Los Angeles: thanks for letting me test out these programs with you. Your enthusiastic participation, gentle critique, and desire for growth shaped this book.

To the interns who worked with me during my 17 years of junior high ministry: Suzanne Meunier, Ralph Barke, Traci Lockman, Chris Logan, Dana Weiler, Heidi Temple, Kent Place, Lisa Froistad, Jeannie Budke, Laura Seapy, Eric Holm, Greg Parker, Tami Holland, Danielle Trundle, and Shannon Lynch. Thanks for investing in the big picture.

To Cathy Smith and Teresa Tulcan, my administrative assistants and friends: thanks for the encouragement, support, and extra miles.

To Linda Colleen Dickie—my wife, teammate, and best friend: thanks for letting me eat chips and salsa on the family room sofa.

To Youth Specialties and all our editors there: thanks for making ministry fun, for believing that I have something to contribute, and for helping me to say it. Special thanks to Sheri Stanley for her willingness to go the extra mile.

To Wade Bass: thanks for the legacy.

God's Not Boring—and Neither Are These Sessions

(or, How to Use *Creative Junior High Programs from A to Z*)

We'll never forget the great insight we received from Calley, an eighth grader in one of our youth programs a number of years ago. "It's a shame," she said, "so many people think God's a drag. He's not, you know. God's not boring."

Calley was right. Very right. God's not boring. One of the greatest tragedies in the history of the Church is that God is often made to seem like a drag. Don't get us wrong—the Christian faith is serious, and times of reverent respect are important. But a relationship with the Creator of the universe is far from boring.

As youth workers we have a wonderful opportunity to help junior high kids discover the passionate, thrilling, wondrous adventure called the Christian life. Sure it's tough, challenging, and sometimes scary, but in no way is it ever boring. At least it's not supposed to be. And that's where we'd like to help.

Our prayer is that you'll take advantage of your position in youth ministry to introduce junior highers to a passionate relationship with Jesus Christ. To help you in your task, we've designed 26 programs (13 in this book, and 13 in *Creative Junior High Programs A to Z, Volume 2*)—programs that communicate life themes in creative, exciting ways. With its alphabetic sequence, the programs are each junior-high sensitive and crammed full of activities, Bible studies, illustrations, and creative alternatives designed to help kids discover our non-boring God.

Try these approaches to the meetings in this book:

 Create a yearlong series.

Use these programs in a year (September through May) as weekly meeting topics. We've tried it, and it's been a big success. Start with A in September or October and finish up with Z in May or June. This plan gives you opportunities to build in some in-between meetings to do something apart from the series, and even a month to insert a three- or four-week subtheme (like a love, sex, and dating series in February).

Darrell: A yearlong plan gives you something to promote to the parents and kids.
Steve: And it will even make you look organized to your pastor. Naturally, needs

change midyear. If you need to change your original schedule, never hesitate to adjust your focus—you can always manipulate a topic title to fit your message.

Darrell: For example, once I—

Steve: I wasn't finished, Darrell.

Darrell: I take it you have more to say?

Steve: The week my group was going to do the letter M and talk about controlling our mouths, the big Northridge earthquake of 1995 hit Los Angeles and creamed my church and many of our homes (including mine). That week I gathered all the students and switched the topic to a discussion on Manic Mountain Moving Motion. That's one lesson they all still remember.

⚛ Let each letter stand on its own.

Don't like the alphabetical approach? Fine. Teach the sessions in any order you like. Or teach just the sessions you like. In any case, you'll find that each session is very different from the others. We really tried to vary our approach.

Steve: I wrote the good sessions.

Darrell: Yeah, right. Don't be a dork. Okay, they're all good. Just keep the kids guessing on what's coming next. They'll love you for your creativity.

⚛ Build things around the letters.

You can do all sorts of creative things for each letter. Try making a huge floor-to-ceiling letter to hang on your wall. (Try this for all 26 letters.) Create a couple of trivia questions that correspond to the week's letter, or give away an off-the-wall prize that begins with the letter of the week (for example, Personal Pan Pizza for P, rock for R, Vicks VapoRub for V—you get the idea).

Here's a weird contest you can do each week. It's called **Can You Throw It?**: Pick out an unusual object that begins with the same letter as your topic and invite several kids from your group to try to throw the object for distance. For example, cheeseburger for C, hula hoop for H, milk carton for M (empty one, please), or a seventh grader for S. Just kidding.

Steve: The more off-the-wall, the better. You'll find the kids looking forward to your meeting to see what they'll be throwing.

Darrell: Weird, but fun.

Use each of these programs to its best effect by—

⚛ Establishing the Big Idea.

The Big Idea rises from a couple questions you need to ask yourself: What is the need of your group, and how can you meet that need? Then establish a goal—which is the Big Idea, the one thing you want your group to grasp through your program. Build your entire program around the purpose of helping your students catch the Big Idea.

Steve: Take extraordinary pains in order to create, institute, and establish this goal, which—considering the complexity of Scripture and its function as a paradigmatic template for human behavi—

Darrell: What he means is this: if you can't articulate your Big Idea simply and clearly, you'll probably have trouble with your meeting.

Now just because we've laid out the Big Ideas for each program in this book, doesn't mean that you can't tweak, adjust, or tailor the Big Ideas—or any components in the sessions themselves—to fit your group better.

Maintaining the flow.

If you're new at running meetings, it's wise to begin with upbeat activities and transition to calmer ones. You want each component of the meeting to set up the next. We've designed this flow into each session. Evaluate the needs of your group and create a flow of program activities that help you achieve your Big Idea.

Changing the order.

We've created a sense of flow in each meeting, with each program component moving smoothly into the next. We understand, however, that our sense of order might be different than yours, so don't hesitate to change things around to fit your group. We don't mind.

Not trying to do it all.

We've included more ideas than you could probably ever use in one meeting. We figure that it's usually better to have loads of options than be stuck with a lot of time and nothing to do. Read through each section and decide what you're going to use and what you're going to eliminate. A tip for beginners: A common mistake is to try to do too much in one session.

Steve: Try to do everything, and you'll only confuse your group.

Darrell: You want them leaving your meeting with a clear picture of your Big Idea.

Adding your own material.

Use our material as a springboard for your own ideas. We think we're pretty creative people, but our stuff may be pretty lame or perhaps too bizarre for you. Dump it and try something new, or improve on our ideas. Creativity is simply giving the status quo a little twist.

Steve: And if an idea bombs, just blame us. Preserve your own credibility at all costs.

Darrell: Or tell them one of the elders suggested the idea to you. After all, it worked in *her* group in 1955.

Planning intentionally.

Does this sound familiar? Five minutes before the meeting, you read the session for the first time and wing it. Sure, we all do it from time to time, but please, please, please don't get too used to it. Our programs are very user-friendly, but if you want them to be great, you've got to prepare. The kids eventually see through a lack of preparation and it will hurt your ministry in the long run. Take care to do a little planning and think through what you're doing. If you're not used to this sort of deliberateness, start with this list:

- **PRAY.** Ask God to give you insight regarding your direction.

- **PLAN.** Lay out an approach to achieve what you want to accomplish.

- **PREVIEW.** Examine the meeting, determine your process, then establish the meeting's Big Idea.

- **PREPARE.** Organize what you need and get ready for the meeting.

- **PARTICIPATE.** Enable maximum involvement from your group.

- **PLAY.** Determine ways to make your meeting enjoyable.

- **PROCEED.** Carry out your meeting.

- **POSTVIEW.** Evaluate the meeting. Did you accomplish your Big Idea?

- **PRAY.** Thank God. Ask for application to be carried out by your kids.

So are you ready to go? We know you'll do a great job and we applaud your willingness to try. Junior high kids need people like you to stick up for them, pray for them, and prove to them that God's not a drag. We believe in you and hope that our project will serve your efforts. After all, God's not boring—so we don't have to be either.

Apathy

Apathy is a dead word—a word without passion or movement; a word that simply lays there, indifferent to all that surrounds it. Apathy says, "I don't care...I don't want to get involved...It doesn't concern me...Just leave me out of it." Everything about apathy runs counter to what God desires for us. On the other hand, the word *commitment* describes all that apathy isn't and all that we should be. We are called to be committed and to live passionately.

Big Idea

God calls us to abandon apathy and pursue commitment.

Key Text • Luke 10:25-37

[25]On one occasion an expert in the law stood up to test Jesus. "Teacher," he asked, "what must I do to inherit eternal life?"

[26]"What is written in the Law?" he replied. "How do you read it?"

[27]He answered: "'Love the Lord your God with all your heart and with all your soul and with all your strength and with all your mind'; and, 'Love your neighbor as yourself.'"

[28]"You have answered correctly," Jesus replied. "Do this and you will live."

[29]But he wanted to justify himself, so he asked Jesus, "And who is my neighbor?"

[30]In reply Jesus said: "A man was going down from Jerusalem to Jericho, when he fell into the hands of robbers. They stripped him of his clothes, beat him and went away, leaving him half dead. [31]A priest happened to be going down the same road, and when he saw the man, he passed by on the other side. [32]So too, a Levite, when he came to the place and saw him, passed by on the other side. [33]But a Samaritan, as he traveled, came where the man was; and when he saw him, he took pity on him. [34]He went to him and bandaged his wounds, pouring on oil and wine. Then he put the man on his own donkey, took him to an inn and took care of him. [35]The next day he took out

two silver coins and gave them to the innkeeper. 'Look after him,' he said, 'and when I return, I will reimburse you for any extra expense you may have.'

³⁶"Which of these three do you think was a neighbor to the man who fell into the hands of robbers?"

³⁷The expert in the law replied, "The one who had mercy on him." Jesus told him, "Go and do likewise."

What You'll Need for This Session

❊ Posterboard or newsprint, markers, and masking tape (see **Before the Meeting**, point 1)
❊ Sheets of paper, markers, and pencils (see **Before the Meeting**, point 2, and **Sub-word Search**, page 16)
❊ Whiteboard (or strips of newsprint and tape) and markers (see **Application**, page 18)
❊ Props for **Spontaneous Role Plays** (page 17)

And if you want to do the options...

❊ Props for **Good Sam** parable (page 18)
❊ Matches and a metal pan, a kid in karate garb, a cardboard casket, darts, or some paint and a paintbrush (see **Abandoning Apathy**, page 19)
❊ Construction paper, markers, and tape (see **Before the Meeting** below, point 5)

Before the Meeting

1. Make two posters by writing APATHY and COMMITMENT on separate pieces of posterboard or newsprint. Tape the posters next to each other on the wall (see **A Charade of Indifference**, page 15 and **Abandoning Apathy**, page 19).

2. Write the individual letters of A-P-A-T-H-Y and C-O-M-M-I-T-M-E-N-T on separate sheets of paper (see **Speed Spell**, page 16).

3. If you don't have a whiteboard, tape up three strips of newsprint for the brainstorming exercise (see **Application**, page 18).

And if you want to do the options...

4. Select four students to act out the **Good Sam** parable (page 18).

5. Make badges out of construction paper that say TOTALLY COMMITTED! for the kids to wear as they leave the meeting. Use a rolled-up piece of masking tape on the back of each badge (see **Abandoning Apathy**, page 19). (Okay, the badges will probably be off and used as ballistic missiles before the kids make it to their parents' cars, but they will make a point.)

A Charade of Indifference

As your start time approaches and kids are drifting in, use your body language and facial expressions to communicate an attitude of indifference to everyone. When kids talk to you, give them an "I-don't-care" response and minimal attention. When you finally pull the group together to begin the meeting, introduce the topic and explain your little charade.

Ask your group: How does it feel to be treated that way?

Then tell them they were experiencing just a little sampling of a distasteful yet common attitude called *apathy*.

Tell the group that you are going to offer them a double-duty-million-dollar-super-stoked word (that's junior high talk as we all know), guaranteed to impress their parents, teachers, and members of the opposite sex. The word is *antithesis*, which literally means the direct opposite. Some examples include light and dark, and good and evil. Refer to your apathy and commitment posters, and explain that throughout the meeting you're going to discuss the antithesis: apathy and commitment.

Share the following stories as examples of how apathy and commitment are opposites. You can also add stories from your personal experience.

✳ **Apathy.** In the early 1970s, the country was shocked by the murder of a young woman in New York City. Though the murder itself was a horrible injustice, what struck the heart of the nation was that the crime took place in full view of several people who chose not to do anything about it. A national news magazine recounted how people ignored the woman's screams, closed their windows, and refused to get involved. The apathy displayed in the situation was devastating.

✳ **Commitment.** On the beach of a Caribbean island is a monument dedicated to three fisherman who gave their lives for another person. The story tells about a fisherman who was being attacked by sharks after his small boat capsized. Seeing the man's plight, another fisherman ran across the sand and into the water to save the other—he was killed by the sharks. A second fisherman entered the water to try to help and he, too, was killed. A third fisherman swam out to help and despite his heroic action, he died with the others. The commitment of these men, who kept trying even when others died before them, is astounding.

Ask your group: Which of these two attitudes is the most appealing? Why?

Share that your goal for this meeting is to challenge the group to move beyond apathy and discover the power of commitment. You're going to accomplish this through a few word games, situation stories, role plays, discussion, and a look at what God has to say about apathy and commitment.

Divide the group into several equal teams and play the following word games.

SUB-WORD SEARCH

Give each team pencils and paper. Their assignment is to see how many sub-words can be created out of the letters in apathy and commitment. The team that gets the most words wins. We came up with the following lists, but there are more. How did you do?

Apathy: At, tap, hat, thy, path, a, pa, yap, pat, ah

Commitment: Come, cone, cot, comet, comment, commit, cent, mitt, mint, moment, men, met, no, not, note, net, tan, ten, tin, tint, tic, tent, ton

SPEED SPELL

Give each team member one of the letters you made from the two words. If you have small groups, give each person more than one letter. The leader calls out a word from the sub-word list. Each team races to spell the word by having those with the correct letters stand and hold up their letters in order. The first team to spell the word gets a point.

Situation Stories

Have the kids remain in their team groups and discuss these situations (You may also bring the whole group together to discuss.):

Ask your group: For each of the following situations, what would be an apathetic response? What would be a committed response?

* *On the way home from school, you see some kids picking on an unpopular kid.*
* *While walking through a parking lot, you see an elderly woman struggling to put groceries in her car.*
* *Your favorite park is always cluttered with trash.*
* *A kid in your youth group can never afford the group activities.*
* *Your neighbor's wall is repeatedly covered with graffiti.*
* *A new kid comes alone to your youth group.*
* *Your pastor appeals to the congregation for help in cleaning the church on Saturday.*
* *You read a story in the paper about a family whose daughter was killed by a drunk driver.*

* *The owner of a convenience store in your neighborhood gives a hard time to kids of a race different than yours.*
* *Your parents are out of town and the lawn needs mowing (or the driveway needs shoveling or the apartment needs straightening).*

Next, invite willing students to come forward and spontaneously act out some of the following scenarios.

SPONTANEOUS ROLE PLAYS

Have your students act out examples of apathy, commitment, or both. You can also gather a few appropriate props for each scene. If you want a few other role-play options, use some of the previous situation stories.

Role-play scenarios:
* Striking up a conversation with a new kid at school.
* Introducing yourself to an elderly neighbor whom you don't know.
* Trying to persuade your dad that you both should go back and give a homeless person you just passed a blanket or a dollar.

Discussion Questions

Take a few minutes to lead your group through these discussion questions.

Ask your group:

* *What is apathy?* (Without feeling or emotion; lack of concern; indifference)
* *What is commitment?* (Obligation, bind, pledge to do something)
* *Why are some people apathetic?* (Fear, shyness, blindness, callousness, lack of resources, easy way out, what can one person do?)
* *Where do you see apathy happening?*
* *What are the results of apathy?*
* *Does the attitude of apathy exist in our youth group?*
* *What is tough about commitment?*
* *What are the results of commitment?*
* *What does God have to say about this topic?*

Scripture Safari

Read the story of the Good Samaritan in Luke 10:25-37.

Ask your group:

❋ *What was the need?*
❋ *Who represented apathy? What did they do?*
❋ *Who represented commitment? What did he do?*

At the end of the meeting, you will be coming back to the closing line of the Good Samaritan story (verse 37), where Jesus challenges the expert in the law to "go and do likewise."

Option

GOOD SAM

Act out the parable of the Good Samaritan. You can have the kids write their own scenarios or set the scene in a modern situation—a young seventh grader is beaten up by some older kids on the way home from school. The school president and the most popular cheerleader both walk by. Then a Christian kid walks by, stops, bandages his wounds, and takes him to the emergency room.

Application

Divide a whiteboard into thirds and write the headings shown below. If you don't have a whiteboard, use three strips of newsprint taped side by side.

Commit to God	**Commit to others**	**Commit to helping others love God**
What can we do?	What can we do?	What can we do?
_____	_____	_____
_____	_____	_____
_____	_____	_____

Ask the group to consider leaving apathy behind to become people dedicated to commitment. Challenge them to pursue the following three areas of commitment: to God, to others, to helping others love God. Explain that commitment must move beyond just thinking about it to actually doing it. They need to put commitment into action.

Following each challenge, spend some time thinking of specific things that you as individuals or as a group can do. Make a list below each point. We've included a few ideas that you can suggest to your group.

THINGS YOUR GROUP CAN DO

* Go to a convalescent hospital and talk with people.
* Help out at a homeless shelter.
* Ride along with a Meals on Wheels program.
* Comfort a sick person.
* Bring flowers to hospital patients.
* Teach a Sunday school class.
* Tutor a younger student.
* Collect food for a food bank.
* Organize a cleanup day at your church.
* Write cards to elderly people in your church.
* Invite someone who is alone to eat lunch with your group at school.
* Paint over graffiti.
* Organize a prayer team for a specific concern or need.
* Make an appointment with your principal, mayor, or pastor to find out what your group can do to make a difference in the school, community, or church.

Conclusion

Abandoning Apathy

Once again refer to your apathy and commitment posters. Ceremoniously destroy the apathy poster—and be creative about how you do it. Here are a few ideas:
* Light it on fire in a metal pan.
* Have a kid dressed in a karate outfit chop and rip it in pieces.
* Place it in a cardboard casket.
* Line up your group and have kids throw darts at it.
* Paint a large X across it.

Then have everyone in the group sign the commitment poster. Hang it in your meeting room throughout the rest of the year as a reminder of your decision to avoid apathy and pursue commitment. Give them their TOTALLY COMMITTED! badges to wear as another reminder.

Make a group pledge (perhaps as you sign the commitment sign) to implement one of your commitment ideas this week. Check back at the next meeting to see how your kids did.

Conclude your time together by going back to the Good Samaritan parable. At the conclusion of the story, Jesus asked the expert in the law who he thought the true neighbor was. The man knew it was the Samaritan—the one who showed mercy. Jesus then responded with four of the most powerful and challenging words in the Bible: "Go and do likewise."

Challenge your group to "go and do likewise."

B

Bummers

Trials, bad times, problems, struggles, frustrations, the blues, the dumps, the total pits—the bummers. While some are huge and ravaging, others can be like mosquitoes—more pestering than devastating. Whether they're traumatic or trivial, bummers can make a mess of our lives. Yet in the midst of the pain, God has something good to say about our hassles.

Big Idea

God can use bummers to make us stronger people.

Key Text • James 1:2-4

²Consider it pure joy, my brothers, whenever you face trials of many kinds, ³because you know that the testing of your faith develops perseverance. ⁴Perseverance must finish its work so that you may be mature and complete, not lacking anything.

What You'll Need for This Session

✳ Sheets of paper, masking tape, and markers a chalkboard or whiteboard (see **Before the Meeting**, point 1)
✳ Three shoe boxes, a Pop Tart, a candy bar, and a jar of baby food or other food items, costumes, and silly prizes for **That's a Bummer** game show (see **Before the Meeting**, point 2)
✳ Suitcase or duffel bag, a half dozen or so heavy objects—dictionaries, hand weights—to fill it with, and a stopwatch (see **Arm Cruncher**, page 26)

And if you want to do the options...

✳ TV, VCR, and the movie *Home Alone*, or some "Roadrunner" cartoons (see **Video Clip**, page 23)
✳ Small pieces of paper, pencils, posterboard, a shoe box, tape, small cross, other symbolic object (depending on which option you do—see **Options**, page 28)

Before the Meeting

1. Write each word of James 1:2-4 on a piece of paper (there are 41 words in the New International Version). Tape each word on a wall in order. You will be pulling key words off the wall throughout the meeting. If you have a chalkboard or whiteboard, you may choose to write the verses on the board.

2. **That's a Bummer** (see page 24) is a spoof on a TV game show. Really ham it up by having an announcer, off-the-wall commercials, a host with a flashy smile and tuxedo, a Vanna-White-in-heels-type assistant, and even some silly prizes. Pick two contestants to play all three rounds, or have two different contestants for each round.

  Label three shoe boxes 1, 2, and 3 and put them on a table. You will place an object under each box for each round of play. Suggestions for objects are given (see **That's a Bummer**, page 24) but feel free to substitute what you'd like. Just make sure that one item in each round is a bummer.

3. Using masking tape, create two lines about twelve feet apart. Designate the area between the lines as the main deck, the right area as the quarter deck, and the left area as the poop deck (see **Poop Deck**, page 26).

4. Ask some of your adult volunteers to be prepared to share a time when they were made stronger through a "bummer" experience (see **Key word 4: Work**, page 27).

And if you want to do the options...

5. Cue up the video tape(s) (see Video Clip, page 23).

6. Prepare items for the **Giving Our Bummers to God** option of your choice (page 28). Write GOD on a shoe box, or make a sign saying, THAT YOU MAY BE MATURE AND COMPLETE, NOT LACKING ANYTHING.

Introduction

Bizarre Bummers

Introduce the meeting by reading a few of these classic true-life bummer situations (excerpted from Shepherd, Kohut and Sweet, *News of the Weird*, New American Library Books, 1989).

❋ The West Virginia highway department built a two-lane bridge for a three-lane section of the state turnpike. A department spokesman blamed designers for the error, which officials didn't notice until the bridge was actually built. "It sounds a lot worse than it is," the spokesman added.

❋ A Swedish business consultant labored 13 years on a book about Swedish economic solutions. He took the 250-page manuscript to be copied, only to have it reduced to 50,000 strips of paper in seconds when a worker confused a copier with a shredder.

※ A cellist with the Soviet Vilnius string quartet was climbing the podium at the 1980 Kuhmo Music Festival for a third round of applause when he tripped and fell on his prized Ruggieri cello, breaking the 300-year-old instrument beyond repair.

※ A train engineer hailed a Gardner, Massachusetts, police officer to say his train had slipped away without him when he left it to buy a candy bar. The two men raced through three towns at breakneck speeds, trying to catch the train at crossings. Meanwhile, the train careened out of control for 30 miles until it was deliberately crashed by dispatchers into a row of empty boxcars.

※ The Army Corp of Engineers inadvertently bulldozed half of an eight-square-mile archaeological site in Delaware containing fossils 80 million years old.

※ A Wisconsin 14-year-old "just lost control" of her toothbrush and swallowed it, but had it retrieved shortly afterward by a doctor. The girl offered only that she was "brushing the back of my tongue because I saw on TV that it helps to get a lot of sugar that way" when "it just slipped and I swallowed it."

※ In New Jersey, a woman was beaten by a mob of sixth graders in 1987 when she visited her son's school dressed as a "Care Bear" on Valentine's day.

※ A Boston sportscaster went to the doctor for an examination to find why he was having trouble hearing. The doctor checked his ear and found a radio ear plug, which had been in his ear for 18 months. Bummer.

Share with the group that these are weird but true stories that happened to real people. While our own bummers are probably not this bizarre, they can still cause turmoil. Tell the group that God has some good advice on how to deal with life's bummers. It's found in James 1:2-4.

Option   **VIDEO CLIP**

Use the scenes from the video *Home Alone* in which the two comic bad guys are trying to break into the house but are outsmarted by the young boy. You can also use clips from "Roadrunner" cartoons where Wile E. Coyote is constantly frustrated by the roadrunner.

Key Words in James 1:2-4

Refer to your James 1:2-4 layout on the wall and tell the group they are going to examine God's good advice by checking out key words from the passage. Pull the paper with each key word off the wall as you discuss it.

Key word 1: Trials

As you pull this key word off the wall—

Ask your group: What are some alternative words for the word **trials**?

Possible answers: bad times, problems, frustrations, struggles, hassles, the blues, the dumps, the pits, eatin' dirt...and bummers.

Play the following **That's a Bummer** game show:

THAT'S A BUMMER

During each round of this game show, the contestants must choose a box (without seeing what's in it) and complete the requirement for that round. It might be enjoyable (everyone cheers) or on the wild (or grody) side (everyone yells in unison "That's a bummer!").

Round 1: Eat (contestant must eat what is under the box)
Box 1: a Pop Tart
Box 2: a Snickers candy bar
Box 3: a jar of Gerber's creamed spinach

Round 2: Say (contestant must say whatever is written on the paper under the box)
Box 1: I am cool and the ultimate person.
Box 2: The rain in Spain falls mainly on the plain.
Box 3: Recite *every other word* of the pledge of allegiance.

Round 3: Do (contestant does whatever is written on the paper under the box)
Box 1: Turn around three times.
Box 2: Do five jumping jacks.
Box 3: Run around the room with both your fingers in your nose.

After the game, explain that while some trials are big ones, others can be small, pesky ones. Both are bummers. Some people might define the difference between big and small bummers differently, but examples of big bummers might include parents fighting or divorce, illness or death, crime, moving to a new town, or getting beat up at school. Examples of small bummers could include not finding matching socks in the morning, a favorite TV program getting preempted, a bad hair day, or ruining your favorite shirt. The bottom line on all bummers is that they can cause all sorts of hassles with our lives.

The passage in James says we will encounter trials of many kinds.

Ask your group: What are some small bummers that you struggled with this week? What are some big bummers that you're facing now or have faced in the past?

Continue on and discover God's good advice on dealing with these problems called bummers.

Key word 2: Joy

As you pull this key word off the wall, explain that there seems to be a tension here in the passage. How can the words *joy* and *trials* be used in the same breath? It sounds almost crazy to say that we should consider it joy when we face trials of many kinds. The understanding comes in realizing there is a difference between joy and happiness.

Ask your group: What is the difference between joy and happiness?

Possible responses: God is not asking us to be happy about our bummers, but rather to allow the joy that Christ has provided to give us hope in the midst of problems. Joy is a deeper emotion that will stand the test of life's bummers. Happiness depends on happenings; joy depends on Jesus.

To illustrate this truth, invite a few volunteers to come up and role-play bummer situations.

ROLE PLAY

Give volunteers one of the following situations and have them spontaneously act out a response that is inappropriately happy. Ask the kids to really ham it up and go wild with the situation.

* Your bicycle gets a flat on the way home from school.
* You step in dog doodoo in your front yard.
* You get a bloody nose during a school speech.
* You leave your math homework at home.

At the conclusion of each role play—

Ask your group: What response would demonstrate the meaning of the phrase "Consider it pure joy when you face trials of many kinds"?

Point out that when the apostle Paul wrote the book of Philippians, he wrote a lot about joy. As a matter of fact, Paul referred to joy or rejoicing 16 times. The amazing thing is that Paul wrote this entire book from a prison cell! He showed us (even modeled) that joy is not dependent on people, things, situations, or circumstances. It remains consistent because God is consistent and faithful.

Key word 3: Perseverance

As you pull this key word off the wall—

Ask your group: How can bummers benefit us?

Possible responses: the reason our Christian joy can remain in the midst of bummers is because trials produce perseverance, a quality of patience, endurance, and steadfastness. This is best illustrated in athletes. Through the discipline and commitment of a tough conditioning program, they strengthen their bodies. In the same way, the very thing that produces pain and struggle (bummers) is what helps build our strength and endurance.

The following two games illustrate this truth. Play them with your group.

ARM CRUNCHER

Take your suitcase or duffel bag filled with heavy objects, and invite kids to come up one at a time and hold the suitcase with their arm completely extended to the side. Time each student and see who can hold his or her arm out the longest.

POOP DECK

Invite your group—or a few volunteers—to stand on the main deck. When you yell "Poop deck!" they must all run to the left area. When you yell "Quarter deck!" they all must run to the right area. When you yell "Main deck!" they all must run to the center area. Yell the commands quickly, so when the group gets to one area, they must quickly run back to another area. After you have done this for a while (and the group is getting pretty tired), start eliminating the last person to get to the designated area. Continue until you have a winner. Interview the winner, commending his or her stamina.

	← length of room or gym →	
"POOP DECK"	"MAIN DECK"	"QUARTER DECK"

Ask your group: What do these games teach us about endurance?

Key word 4: Work

Read verse 4 and pull the word WORK off the wall. Perseverance will finish its work—we will be more mature and complete, not lacking anything.

Then share the following illustration with your group:

When Dave was 16, he learned that his parents were going to divorce. It was devastating. The pain was great, but Dave remained consistent in his commitment to grow in his relationship with God. Even though it was hard, he worked at dealing with the situation. By the time Dave turned 20, he was a leader in his church and working with the high school youth group. One evening with the group, 16-year-old Bernadette shared how she had just found out that her parents were filing for divorce. Tearfully, the young woman shared her pain and her fears. The group encouraged her, but it was the insight and wisdom of one person who brought her the most comfort. This person spoke with an incredible sense of compassion and understanding. It was Dave. Even though God hates divorce, he used the pain of that situation to build strength within Dave. This strength eventually enabled him to meet the needs of others with similar pain.

Say to your group: Bummers produce perseverance and perseverance produces a good work, that we may be mature and complete, not lacking anything.

Ask your adult volunteers to share situations in which they were made stronger through bummers, big or small.

Memorization

As a reminder that God can use our bummers to make us better people, challenge the group to memorize James 1:2-4 and say it to themselves each time they face a bummer this week. Point out that the passage indicates *when*, not *if*, they will face trials. Help them memorize the verse with the following exercise.

MEMORY EXERCISE

Refer back to the verses on the wall. You have already pulled off four key words from the passage. Have the group read the passage with the missing key words. Next, remove two more words and say it again. Keep removing words and quoting the passage. When the wall is blank, group members should be able to say the verse from memory.

Giving Our Bummers to God

Here are three ways you could end this session.

Options

YOU COULD...

Give everyone a small sheet of paper and a pencil. Ask them to write down bummers they are struggling with. Take your shoe box with GOD written on the side, and invite students to put their bummers in the box to symbolize giving them to God.

OR YOU COULD...

Close the meeting as described above. Then, after some weeks or months (or years?), mail the papers back to the students with James 1:2-4 written on the back of each envelope:

> Consider it pure joy, my brothers, whenever you face trials of many kinds, because you know that the testing of your faith develops perseverance. Perseverance must finish its work so that you may be mature and complete, not lacking anything.

OR MAYBE EVEN...

Have the students write out their bummers on paper, fold the papers over, and tape them to a wall (or even a small cross). Once everyone has finished, place over the sheets of paper a sign that states THAT YOU MAY BE MATURE AND COMPLETE, NOT LACKING ANYTHING.

Changes

Changes are tough, often unwanted, but sometimes necessary. You'd think junior high students would love change—after all, they're in the middle of some big changes themselves. But maybe that's why they actually resist change more than anyone else. Part of growing up and becoming an adult is learning to embrace change, good or bad, and that's what this program is all about.

Big Idea

Changes in life are appropriate and helpful, even when they're uncomfortable.

Key Text • Numbers 13:26-33

[26]They came back to Moses and Aaron and the whole Israelite community at Kadesh in the Desert of Paran. There they reported to them and to the whole assembly and showed them the fruit of the land. [27]They gave Moses this account: "We went into the land to which you sent us, and it does flow with milk and honey! Here is its fruit. [28]But the people who live there are powerful, and the cities are fortified and very large. We even saw descendants of Anak there. [29]The Amalekites live in the Negev; the Hittites, Jebusites and Amorites live in the hill country; and the Canaanites live near the sea and along the Jordan."

[30]Then Caleb silenced the people before Moses and said, "We should go up and take possession of the land, for we can certainly do it."

[31]But the men who had gone up with him said, "We can't attack those people; they are stronger than we are." [32]And they spread among the Israelites a bad report about the land they had explored. They said, "The land we explored devours those living in it. All the people we saw there are of great size. [33]We saw the Nephilim there (the descendants of Anak come from the Nephilim). We seemed like grasshoppers in our own eyes, and we looked the same to them."

What You'll Need for This Session

❋ Three white bed sheets and 12 diaper pins (see **Diaper Game**, page 30)
❋ TV, VCR, and two *Edge TV* segments: "McLane Goes to Africa" (Vol. 1) and

"McLane Escapes with His Life" (Vol. 3) available from Youth Specialties (see **Video Clip 1** and **2**, pages 31 and 32)

❋ Several stalks of grain (preferably actual wheat) and 3 kinds of wheat cereal: a plain one (like Shredded Wheat), a little fancier one (like Frosted Mini-Wheats), and a fancy one (like Raisins in the Middle—see **Cereal Morph**, page 32)

Before the Meeting

1. Ask a relatively new baby and one of the baby's parents if they could help start off this youth meeting (see **Ready for Change**, below. If you don't know anyone who's recently had a baby, just check around—people have them all the time).

2. Do something radically different with your room setup for this meeting: Turn the chairs to face the other way, put them in a spiral instead of a semi-circle, etc. Also, dress differently than usual—casual if you are normally dressed up, etc. Deviate from your normal group meeting as much as you can.

3. Cue up the videos (see **Video Clip 1** and **2**, pages 31 and 32).

Introduction

Ready for Change

Explain to your group that you're tired of the status quo—you're ready for something new and different. You're ready for change! As you speak, have a new mom or dad walk into the room with their relatively young baby. Junior high students (even the boys) love seeing infants; they'll enjoy the visit.

   Have the parent say something like, "I understand someone in here needs to experience a change—well, our baby can certainly provide that!" Have the parent illustrate, with their baby, how to correctly change a diaper (good baby-sitting skill here). When they're done, have some fun showing the baby around again and thank the parent as he or she leaves. Continue on this subject by playing the following game.

DIAPER GAME

Choose six people for a diaper-changing competition. Pair them up, then give each team a sheet and four diaper pins. Designate who the "diapee" is, then give the teams three minutes to see who can do the best job diapering their partner—without sticking them with pins. Let the rest of the kids vote on the best diaper job.

Talk briefly about changes in life—how some are good, some not so good, but often, just like the baby's diapers, are necessary. Ask if anyone has undergone tough changes in their lives within the last year: divorce, move, school change, etc. Have them share what it was like. Ask other students to share upcoming changes about which they are apprehensive. What fears do they have? Continue to illustrate change with this next game.

CONCENTRATION

Place your chairs in a circle with one extra chair to the left of the leader. The game is based on a simple rhythmic pattern of 1-2-3-4. On beat one, everyone slaps their thighs, on beat two, everyone claps their hands, on beat three, everyone snaps their left fingers, on beat four, everyone snaps their right fingers.

The game begins with the leader establishing the beat and the group repeating the rhythm several times through. After the group has the rhythm established, the leader calls out his or her own name on beat three, then one of the students' names on beat four. The student whose name was called waits until the next sequence to do the same thing: call his own name on beat three, and another student's name on beat four. The process repeats until someone misses saying the two names on the right beats. This is the easy part!

As soon as a person misses the rhythm, he or she moves to the chair to the immediate left of the leader. Everyone sitting between the now-open spot and the leader moves one seat to their left. If the leader misses the rhythm, he or she moves to the end of the line and is replaced by the number two person to the right, who now begins the next round.

Here's the catch—when everyone changes chairs, they must adopt the name of whoever was previously sitting in *that* chair. When someone calls that name during the game, the person sitting in the chair responds, *not* the person whose name it really is. The fun comes in trying to adjust to your name change. It's not easy— you have to be able to remember your new name for each round.

Video Clip 1

When you've finished the game, show the segment "McLane Goes to Africa" from *Edge TV* (Vol 1.). It's about a high school student whose parents have decided to take the family on a short-term mission to Africa for a couple of years. McLane talks about his struggles, fears, and feelings. It's an interesting clip with a strong, humorous angle junior highers will like.

After the video is over, break the group up into several small groups.

Discuss the following questions:
❋ *How would you feel if you were in McLane's shoes?*
❋ *Would you rebel against your parent's decision or be excited about it? Why?*

Scripture Safari

Ask the group to turn to Numbers 13:26-33. Read the story of the Israelites' great exploration of the Promised Land and the report of the scouts who were overwhelmed by what they found.

Ask your group:
❋ *Why were the scouts so reluctant to go into the Promised Land?*
❋ *What was their view of themselves in relation to the people they discovered?*
❋ *Who were the individuals that wanted to take over the land?*
❋ *What was their argument for doing so?*
❋ *What do you think God wanted the people to do?*

Video Clip 2

Show the segment from *Edge TV* (Vol. 3) that updates McLane's situation. Then wrap up by telling kids that even though changes in life can be difficult, they are often necessary—and even good for us.

Conclusion

Cereal Morph

Pull out your stalks of grain and the boxes of cereal. Show each item one by one. The stalks of grain are good to eat, but not without some preparation. Shredded Wheat makes the grain easier to eat, but it's still pretty boring. Next, try the Frosted Mini-Wheats. They may not be the best food on the planet, but they sure are more fun to eat than stalks of wheat and Shredded Wheat. But they started with simple Shredded Wheat, and became something really great through changes.

Conclude by looking at Raisins in the Middle. What's next? What changes will the cereal makers do next? Well, the changes might be good or bad, but you can be certain of this: There will be change! Just be ready for it!

Close in prayer, asking God to help you all as the world around you changes. Pray with "popcorn" prayers—students say one-word prayers after you start with a sentence. For example:

Leader: Lord, we all struggle with changes, particularly in these areas of our lives…
Students: Home…School…My friends…Brothers…My math teacher…etc.

Dating

The world of dating stirs up a myriad of emotions. Like a roller coaster ride, the dating adventure creates thrills for some and chills in others. The junior high years provide kids with a great opportunity to build a solid foundation on how to approach dating in the years to come. God had wonderful things in mind when he created relationships, and choosing to follow his good advice is the wisest thing we can do.

Big Idea

We can prepare for dating in the future by building

our inner character now.

Key Text· Luke 6:48-49

[48] "He is like a man building a house, who dug down deep and laid the foundation on rock. When a flood came, the torrent struck that house but could not shake it, because it was well built. [49]But the one who hears my words and does not put them into practice is like a man who built a house on the ground without a foundation. The moment the torrent struck that house, it collapsed and its destruction was complete."

What You'll Need for This Session

❈ A stage or curtain, and an offstage microphone or two (see **The First Dance**, page 34)
❈ Pencils and paper (see **Panel discussions 1** and **2**, pages 36-37)
❈ Copies of **Character Builder #1** or **Character Builder #2** puzzles (pages 41 and 42)
❈ Copies of **The Dating Standard Emblems** (pages 44 and 45)

Before the Meeting

1. Find four actors from your youth group (two males and two females) for **The First Dance** ad-lib skit (page 34); one or two run-throughs are helpful, but this sketch can be done impromptu with a creative couple onstage.

About the Big D and Junior Highers

Talking about dating to a junior high/middle school crowd is a delicate task. While it's an important issue to address, the topic creates dilemmas. First, junior high boys are generally less mature than junior high girls. The difference between an eighth-grade girl and a seventh-grade boy can seem like 30 years. Second, the majority of the kids have not (and probably should not have) begun dating yet. Third, many parents (especially those with their first junior higher) are nervous about you discussing this topic.

Should we still talk about dating with junior highers? The answer is yes. When you do, consider splitting the guys and girls for all or much of the session. This will allow you to focus the lesson to their varied maturity levels. And even though most junior highers have not begun dating, they are very aware of the opposite sex. We have a wonderful opportunity to help them prepare for the future.

Finally, parents need to understand that you're merely giving kids a handle on how to deal with what's to come. The world is bombarding preteens and teens with a dating message that isn't healthy. Youth leaders and parents working together can provide kids with a godly perspective.

A final word of wisdom: While some in your group may have begun dating (and are very experienced), others may still be in the cootie stage. Customize your discussions, skits, and activities to your particular group.

LEADER HINT

It may be wise to send a letter to parents explaining why you're talking about dating from the junior high perspective. This will help parents see that you're not trying to grow their kids up too soon. This letter can help parents see you as partners with them in meeting the needs of their children.

Introduction

The First Dance

Introduce the meeting with this fun skit about dating. It will serve as a catalyst for everyone to laugh off nervous energy and focus on the topic at hand.

This is a simple ad-lib skit of a guy and a girl going to their first school dance. The gimmick is that another guy and girl are offstage (or behind a curtain) and do the entire narration as the "thoughts" of the two actors on stage. The two actors act out the events without saying a word as the voices behind

LEADER HINT

This session is merely a glance into the window of dating—an introduction into the world of guy/girl relationships. The majority of the session will be spent in a discussion time called "Wise Words for Wise Women and Wise Guys." It will allow for spontaneous discussion so be sure to leave ample time for it—you might consider extending this topic over more than one session to get into deeper issues.

the stage provide the ad-lib "thoughts." The two actors onstage act out getting ready for the dance, going to the dance, checking everyone out, getting the nerve to ask—or the fear of not getting asked—to dance, and the actual dance. Have fun with the ad-lib.

Say to your group: Relationships between guys and girls can be pretty amazing. While they're fairly easy and natural for some, they can be pretty scary and threatening for the rest of us. Let's take a look at this thing called dating.

Two Big Truths about the Big D

Truth 1: God is into relationships.

Remind the group of the Army recruiting slogan: BE ALL THAT YOU CAN BE. The slogan suggests that the Army can help people fulfill their greatest potential.

Ask your group: What are some things that can make us better people?

After the group has offered their ideas, share that God is very creative in the ways he shapes us into better people. One of his favorite ways is to use other people. The bottom line: God thinks relationships are good for us because they help us grow.

1. Others help us grow.
Read Proverbs 27:17.

Ask your group: How can relationships help sharpen us?

2. We help others grow.
Read Hebrews 10:24.

Ask your group: How can we spur one another on toward love and good deeds through relationships?

Truth 2: We need to build a firm foundation before we date.

Because God uses relationships to help us grow, we should take great care to build our relationships on a solid foundation. If we take care now, we will see positive results in the future. If we fail to take care now, we can expect to see negative results in the future.

Read Luke 6:48-49, then—

Ask your group:
❋ *What are examples of building relationships on sand?*
❋ *What are examples of building relationships on rock?*

After they suggest some answers—

Say to your group: With this in mind, let's spend some time talking about how we keep our dating relationships on solid ground.

Wise Words for Wise Women and Wise Guys

At this point in the meeting, have the guys and girls head off to separate rooms for a discussion. This will allow you to focus on the unique needs of both sexes and their maturity levels. Tell the girls you have some wise words for wise women and tell the guys you have some wise words for wise guys.

This is the main focus of the meeting, so be sure to leave yourself plenty of time for good discussion.

Panel discussion 1

Male panel leaders go with junior high boys, and female panel leaders go with junior high girls. Use one of the options below to provide a time where the junior highers can hear from the panel leaders about dating and the opposite sex.

Questions from kids

Pass out paper and pencils and invite the group to write out questions they have about the opposite sex. Have one of the panel discussion leaders read the questions, and all leaders provide answers and foster further discussion.

Generic questions

Have panel discussion leaders use some of these basic questions to trigger discussion:
* How do girls/guys like to be treated?
* How do you approach a girl/guy you'd like to meet?
* What do girls/guys like to talk about?
* What do you do when a girl/guy ignores you?
* How do you know if a girl/guy likes you?
* What's the best way to tell a girl/guy you like them?
* What do you do if you are really shy?
* What do girls/guys like and not like about the opposite sex?
* What do you do when you like someone but he/she likes someone else?
* What do you do when someone likes you, but you don't like him/her?
* Can you just be friends with a girl/guy?
* Is it okay not to have a boyfriend/girlfriend?
* How do girls/guys want us to act with them?

Panel discussion 2

Switch your leaders. Have male panel leaders go with the junior high girls and the female panel leaders go with the junior high boys. This is a great opportunity for the leaders to give the girls' and guys' perspectives on the opposite sex. Again, invite the kids to ask their own questions, write out their questions, or use the set of questions listed above.

LEADER HINT

This session is merely an introduction into the dating world. Depending on your group, you may want to go deeper into other areas. Check out your local Christian bookstore for some of the great books on this topic. Here are a couple of good ones to get you started:
* What Hollywood Won't Tell You about Sex, Love and Dating, by Susie Shellenberger and Greg Johnson, Regal Books, 1994.
* Getting Ready for the Guy-Girl Thing, by Susie Shellenberger and Greg Johnson, Regal Books, 1991.

Getting Ready for Relationships

At this point, bring both groups together.

Say to your group: It's great to have wise people to help us understand dating. It can be a pretty crazy world out there, and we need the good advice of people with experience to help us through. Now let's look at some good advice God has about preparing for dating relationships.

1. Be yourself.

Read 1 Samuel 16:7.

> But the Lord said to Samuel, "Do not consider his appearance or his height, for I have rejected him. The Lord does not look at the things man looks at. Man looks at the outward appearance, but the Lord looks at the heart."

Say to your group: Who we are on the inside is pretty special, and that's what we want people to see. When we try to act like someone we're not, it usually catches up with us in the long run. Besides that, there's loads of stress in trying to fake it. Let's give ourselves and the people around us a dose of peace by just being ourselves. The best us is the <u>real</u> us.

2. Be a person of character.

Read Psalm 84:11.

> For the Lord God is a sun and shield; the Lord bestows favor and honor; no good thing does he withhold from those whose walk is blameless.

Ask your group: What is character?

After they suggest some answers—

Say to your group: The dictionary defines <u>character</u> as "the complex of mental and ethical traits marking a person." Basically, it's what we are on the inside that makes and shapes our attitudes and actions. If we work on our insides, it will produce results on the outside. Let's build our characters, and we'll be way ahead in the dating arena.

CHARACTER PUZZLES

Pass out either Character Builder #1 (page 41) or Character Builder #2 (page 42) to the group and invite them to look for the 30 character traits hidden in the letters. Character Builder #1 is pretty easy (no diagonal words, but some are backwards) and Character Builder #2 is a little more difficult (diagonal and backwards-diagonal words). The solutions are on page 43.

3. Be kind.
Read 2 Timothy 2:24.

> And the Lord's servant must not quarrel; instead, he must be kind to everyone, able to teach, not resentful.

Say to your group: Some of us—especially males—think that we have to be rude and obnoxious to be cool in relationships. That's just plain stupid. Rudeness to the opposite sex is often a sign of insecurity about who we are on the inside. As we build our character, let's try being kind. Being known as a kind person makes us big-time winners in the long run. It's cool to be kind and sharp people prefer it.

4. Be an encourager.
Read Job 4:4.

> Your words have supported those who stumbled; you have strengthened faltering knees.

Say to your group: Words can knock us off our feet. But according to this powerful sentence spoken to Job, words can also keep us standing strong. One of the greatest gifts we can give someone in a dating relationship is a strong view of him or herself. Let's be encouragers and lift up those whom we date.

5. Be a God seeker.
Read Matthew 6:33.

> But seek first his kingdom and his righteousness, and all these things will be given to you as well.

Say to your group: Our first goal is to love God and grow in our relationships with him. If dating relationships take priority over our relationships with God, then we're missing the main point. God created others and uses them in our lives to help us grow. If we exclude God from our dating, then we're out of sync with his wonderful plan for us. A boyfriend or a girlfriend can't meet needs that only Jesus can fill. Let's develop our relationships with God, and then let him be at the center of our dating relationships.

Conclusion

Creating a Dating Standard

Challenge the group to consider setting up a dating standard.

In old times, a standard was a conspicuous object (such as an emblem or banner) placed on top of a pole to mark a rallying point, especially in a battle. The significance and power of the emblem gave a reference point for all to see. In modern times, our standards can be values and convictions that we rally around in our lives.

DATING STANDARD EMBLEMS

Invite kids to create their own personal standards to carry into their dating lives. Pass out the **Dating Standard Emblems** found on pages 44 and 45. The first standard enables students to write their commitments as letters to God. The second standard allows them to write their commitments in four separate parts.

Have them write, in their own words, prayers expressing their commitment to keep God in the center of their dating relationships. Tell kids to pull out their standards and read them before each date they have.

A note from Steve: Creating a dating standard before you actually start dating really does work. I know, because I did it. When I began dating, I pulled out the emblem I had made a few years earlier and renewed my commitment to God in my relationship life. Yes, I struggled at times, but I kept God at the center of my relationships all the way through dating and engagement, and into marriage. The pressure from the world will be pretty tough, but God does know what he's talking about and wants us to trust him with everything—even our dating lives.

Close in prayer. Have your kids dedicate (individually or as a group) their dating lives to God.

LEADER HINT

After the meeting, spend some significant time in prayer for each of your kids. Ask God to protect them in their future relationships.

Character Builder #1

Directions: Words are either horizontal or vertical (not diagonal),
and may be spelled either forwards or backwards.

```
H X L U F I C R E M W X R S L P A W
H G R A T E F U L P O I S E D U S R
R I G D P A T I E N T D Q R Z N U E
R Y D L U F H T U R T P R L Q D O L
I Y N Z G J F W Q Y Y R Q U O E E T
V Z I C L A Y O L J L A B F P R T N
G I K O O F L U K Z D Y F H D S R E
E A R E R C N I S N E O T E T U G
S P I R I T U A L S E R R I N A O J
P U R E E L B M U H I F G A I N C M
G N I V O L U O P C R U I F L D W L
E U T H A N K F U L F L V G P I I U
S R E S P O N S I B L E I I I N L F
I O F I N T E G R I T Y N Q C G U E
W S S E L F L E S V X O G Z S I F C
C O M P A S S I O N A T E L I T Y A
E L B A T I P S O H F Z S F D V O E
E B U Z Y H J C H E E R F U L W J P
```

WORD LIST

cheerful

compassionate

courteous

disciplined

faithful

forgiving

friendly

gentle

grateful

hospitable

humble

integrity

joyful

kind

loving

loyal

merciful

patient

peaceful

poised

prayerful

pure

responsible

selfless

sincere

spiritual

thankful

truthful

understanding

wise

Character Builder #2

Directions: Words may be spelled horizontally, vertically, or diagonally—
and either forwards or backwards.

```
G C M B G Q S N A O R R E W O D D
N H Y L D N E I R F Q M J Z Q Z P
D E N I L P I C S I D R Y O O A E
X E L M G M L V N S E C H G T H C
X R A B N H U E I B E G K I C D N
Y F U S I O F T I G G L E H U L D
F U T I V S K A P N R N F N M O D
E L I U O P N N M E T O D L T R D
P U R D L I A O F E A E F V E L Y
X F I O A T H I P A R C G W I S E
S Y P X Y A T S K S I C E R O S U
K O S Z O B I S T U E T I F I N A
S J D X L L H A L N X R H F U T L
U Z P U R E N P R A Y E R F U L Y
P O I S E D T M T R U T H F U L T
W M S P I N C O U R T E O U S L A
N C Q N S I N C E R E L B M U H A
I D G T Z K V E P L U F E T A R G
```

WORD LIST

cheerful
compassionate
courteous
disciplined
faithful
forgiving
friendly
gentle
grateful
hospitable

humble
integrity
joyful
kind
loving
loyal
merciful
patient
peaceful
poised

prayerful
pure
responsible
selfless
sincere
spiritual
thankful
truthful
understanding
wise

SOLUTIONS

Character Builder #1

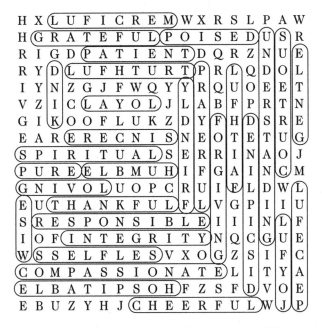

Character Builder #2

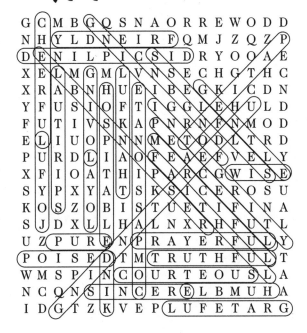

These puzzles were created with the computer program Ultra Find and Circle, which is about $35 from Software Singularity, P.O. Box 2106, Greer, SC 29652-2106. A great tool for youth workers!

Dating Standard Emblem

Dear God,

Your Loving Child

_____

Dating Standard Emblem

Encouragement

We all remember the classic chant we used to say as kids: "Sticks and stones may break my bones, but words will never hurt me." It didn't take long before we realized that the phrase didn't tell the truth—words *do* hurt. By the same token, kind words build us up—and we need that encouragement. When we're feeling mashed and trashed, bruised and broken, or low and slow, words that build up are precious.

Big Idea

It's better to build people up than to tear them down.

Key Texts • 1 Thessalonians 5:11-23

[11]Therefore encourage one another and build each other up, just as in fact you are doing.

[12]Now we ask you , brothers, to respect those who work hard among you, who are over you in the Lord and who admonish you. [13]Hold them in the highest regard in love because of their work. Live in peace with each other. [14]And we urge you, brothers, warn those who are idle, encourage the timid, help the weak, be patient with everyone. [15]Make sure that nobody pays back wrong for wrong, but always try to be kind to each other and to everyone else.

[16]Be joyful always; [17]pray continually; [18]give thanks in all circumstances, for this is God's will for you in Christ Jesus.

[19]Do not put out the Spirit's fire; [20]do not treat prophecies with contempt. [21]Test everything. Hold on to the good. [22]Avoid every kind of evil.

[23]May God himself, the God of peace, sanctify you through and through. May your whole spirit, soul and body be kept blameless at the coming of our Lord Jesus Christ.

Ephesians 4:29-32

[29]Do not let any unwholesome talk come out of your mouths, but only

(continued)

what is helpful for building others up according to their needs, that it may benefit those who listen. [30]And do not grieve the Holy Spirit of God, with whom you were sealed for the day of redemption. [31]Get rid of all bitterness, rage and anger, brawling and slander, along with every form of malice. [32]Be kind and compassionate to one another, forgiving each other, just as in Christ God forgave you.

Romans 1:11-12

[11]I long to see you so that I may impart to you some spiritual gift to make you strong—[12]that is, that you and I may be mutually encouraged by each other's faith.

Hebrews 10:24-25

[24]And let us consider how we may spur one another on toward love and good deeds. [25]Let us not give up meeting together, as some are in the habit of doing, but let us encourage one another—and all the more as you see the Day approaching.

What You'll Need for This Session

✳ Trash can, masking tape, and a Nerf basketball (see **Before the Meeting**, point 1)
✳ Two plastic marker cones (available at most sporting goods stores, see **Before the Meeting**, point 2)
✳ Golf putter, golf ball, scissors, and a shoe box (see **Before the Meeting**, point 3)
✳ Paper in assorted colors, drawing paper, and markers (see **Before the Meeting**, point 4)
✳ Sheets of paper, pens, and tape (see **Backslapper**, page 50)
✳ Whiteboard or newsprint and markers (see **The Power of Words**, page 50, and **Scripture Safari**, page 52)
✳ Dictionary, a few preselected words, or the suggested word list, pencils and paper (see **Team Dictionary**, page 51)
✳ Set of toy building blocks or some small cardboard boxes (see **Build-ups and Tear-downs Exercise**, page 52)
✳ Cassette or CD *Sticks and Stones* by Wes King (Reunion Records) and cassette/CD player (see **Reflection**, page 52)

Before the Meeting

1. Set up a trash can and mark off a free-throw line with masking tape (see **Trash Can Shoot**, below).

2. Set up one plastic marker cone and mark off a shooting line five feet away (see **Cone Flip**, below).

3. Cut an arch in the shoe box and make a putting line with masking tape (see **Golf Putt**, below).

4. For **Team Picture Game** (page 51) you'll need a set of the same 10 words (each word on a separate sheet) for each team that plays. So decide how many teams you'll use (maybe three to five on a team) and select 10 sheets of colored paper for each team—a different color for each team. Choose your own 10 words or use the following:

skateboard	attitude
homework	CD
video	maturity
bubble gum	fad
rock 'n' roll	put-downs.

Introduction

Shoot, Throw, Putt—with Encouragement

As the group arrives, have a few games ready that can provide opportunities to encourage the kids. Set up three stations in your meeting area and assign a staff member to lead each game. The leader's job is to offer encouragement to any student who tries his or her event. Have staff leaders use the opportunity to offer bold, encouraging words to each person.

TRASH CAN SHOOT

Invite kids to take shots from your free-throw line with a Nerf basketball. See who can make the most shots in a row.

CONE FLIP

Have kids step up to the line and attempt to throw a plastic marker cone, with an underhand back-flip toss, onto a stationary marker cone. Give points for the most out of five attempts, ten, etc.

GOLF PUTT

Kids try to putt a golf ball down a tape line into your arched shoe box.

After the games, gather the group together for the following crowdbreaker.

BACKSLAPPER

Tape a piece of paper to each person's back. Give everyone a pen, and have them mingle, writing compliments and encouragements on each other's backs. At the end of the activity, have everyone pair up with someone else. Each person reads the other person's sheet.

This activity carries some risk, especially with junior highers. Make sure your leaders are wandering around and watching for people who are getting missed. If you don't think this activity will work with your group, skip it and open with the next activity.

The Power of Words

Write this children's saying on a whiteboard (you'll refer to it later in the meeting, too): STICKS AND STONES WILL BREAK MY BONES BUT NAMES WILL NEVER HURT ME.

Ask your group:
✳ *Do you think this is a true or false statement? Why?*
✳ *How can words hurt us?*
✳ *How can words encourage us?*

Have the group sing the song "Home on the Range." Go ahead and have fun—sing it tongue-in-cheek with a cowboy twang. Here are the words:

> Oh, give me a home,
> Where the buffalo roam
> And the deer and the antelope play.
> Where seldom is heard
> A discouraging word,
> And the skies are not cloudy all day.

Play off the "discouraging word" phrase. Tell the group that there are discouraging words as well as encouraging words. By definition, a word is "one or a sequence of speech sounds having meaning and making up an independent linguistic unit" (impress your group with that phrase). For such little things, words can wield mighty blows—people have died for them…nations have been built around them…in one swift stroke, words can build up or tear down.

Next, we'll have some fun with words.

TEAM PICTURE GAME

Divide the group into your predetermined number of teams. Give each team some drawing paper and a pen or pencil. Place each team's set of words (the ones you prepared beforehand) across the room from the teams. Be sure to shuffle the order of the words in each stack so teams won't be drawing the same words at the same time.

When the game begins, the first player from each team runs to her stack of words, glances at the first word, runs back to her team, and draws the word, *using only pictures* (no talking or writing letters/numbers allowed). When the team guesses the correct word, the next person on that team runs to the stack, glances at the second word, and returns to the team to draw. The teams repeat this process until they have gone through their entire stack of words. The first team to complete their stack wins.

TEAM DICTIONARY GAME

Have the students remain in their teams. Read an outrageous word to the group and ask each team to create a fake but believable definition for the word. Have teams write down their definitions and turn them in. Read the fake definitions along with the real definition (without telling the teams which one is the real definition). Each team votes for the definition they think is the real one. If a team guesses the correct definition, they get three points. If a team guesses a fake definition, the team who *wrote* that definition gets two points. Here are a few fun words that you may use, with their dictionary definitions (or, grab a dictionary and find a few of your own):

* hurdy-gurdy—a stringed musical instrument
* kerf—the cut in a tree made by a saw
* paternoster—The Lord's Prayer
* tiglon—a hybrid between a male tiger and a female lion.
* oologist—a collector of birds' eggs.
* deasil—clockwise
* widdershins—counterclockwise
* yurt—a Mongolian tent
* nux vomica—the poisonous seed of an Asian tree

Build-ups and Tear-downs Exercise

Ask your group: What are words or phrases that build up or encourage others?

As kids share encouraging words and phrases, place a building block for each word or phrase in front of the group. Keep stacking blocks on top of each other as they share their encouraging words and phrases.

Ask your group: What are words or phrases that tear down or discourage others?

As kids share, remove a building block from the stack for each discouraging word or phrase. Keep removing blocks as tear-down words and phrases are shared. (As an alternative, when the first tear-down phrase is shared, you can choose to dramatically knock all the blocks down, noting that it takes only one discouraging word to tear someone down.)

Reflection

Now point out what's written on the whiteboard (or wherever): STICKS AND STONES WILL BREAK MY BONES BUT NAMES WILL NEVER HURT ME. Then play the Wes King song "Sticks and Stones" from the Reunion album of the same name.

Scripture Safari

Now read 1 Thessalonians 5:11-23.

Say to your group: Let's list ways we could put these verses into practice.

Use a whiteboard or newsprint to create the following chart.

VERSE	WHAT TO DO	WAYS TO APPLY IT
11	Therefore encourage one another and build each other up.	Encourage a friend who did poorly on his math test.

Now read Ephesians 4:29-32. Ask, "What are we commanded to get rid of? What do we replace it with? How has God set an example for us?"

Read Romans 1:11-12 and Hebrews 10:24-25. Ask, "Why do we need encouragement from one another? Is it easier to give or receive encouragement? How do we encourage others without looking like we're trying to get something in return?"

Application

Ask your group: How would you encourage the people in the following situations:
* *A brother or sister who is struggling in school*
* *A friend whose parents are getting a divorce*
* *A teacher who has a hard time with discipline*
* *A coach whose team always loses*
* *Your mom or dad when she or he is lonely*
* *Your mom or dad after a hard day at work*
* *A neighbor who lives alone*
* *A teammate whose mistake just lost the game for the team*
* *A classmate who is about to give a speech*
* *A friend who comes to school wearing a new outfit*
* *An unpopular person at school*

Tell this story to your group:

In Bakersfield, California, a teacher challenged his class to make a radical difference in their world by committing random acts of kindness and senseless acts of beauty. The students took to the task and began to do amazing acts of encouragement—for no reason at all. Soon their efforts caught on and began to sweep the community—and then the country.

Say to your group: *We often tear down others in an attempt to build ourselves up. If we need to feel good, let's build up others. It will be contagious. Let's commit our own random acts of kindness and senseless acts of beauty.*

Does your group want some examples? Good! We just happened to have listed some.

Random acts of kindness and senseless acts of beauty your group can try:
* Stand in front of a mall or grocery store and open the door for people for an hour.
* Get up early some Saturday and wash the next-door neighbor's car.
* Stop by a nursing home after school and chat with people.
* Make a sack lunch for a homeless person.
* Show up at the local police or fire station with a box of cookies or doughnuts.
* Offer to paint over graffiti at a local business.

❋ Clean up your sister's room while she's gone.
❋ Call your mom or dad at work and thank them for working so hard to support you.
❋ Wait for the mailman or garbage man with a soda or cup of coffee.
❋ Think of a store employee who is always nice. Go in and tell her boss what a good employee she is.
❋ Pick up trash at a neighborhood park.
❋ Make a conscious decision to smile at people for a day.

Nothing wild, just a few simple things junior high kids can do when they put their minds to it.

Conclusion

Encouragers Anonymous

Here are three options for ending this session:

Options

YOU COULD...

Place the names of your group members in a box. Have each person draw a name and anonymously do encouraging things for that person during the next month.

OR YOU COULD...

Choose a family in your church who's going through a rough time. Ask your group to commit to doing encouraging things for them for a month. The family doesn't need to know your identity.

OR MAYBE...

Ask the group members to commit to doing "random acts of kindness and senseless acts of beauty" (suggestions on page 53) during the following week. They can report their results at the next meeting.

Follow-up

Over the next couple of weeks, mail a postcard to every kid at the meeting, offering a brief word of encouragement.

LEADER HINT

Make it a habit to send kids encouraging notes. Use cardstock paper and design creative postcards, or keep an eye out for some that are off the wall. Try adding creative clip art or paste-up cartoons to the cards. When you write, keep it simple—nothing lengthy—just let the kids know you think they're great.

Friendships

God never intended for us to go it alone—that's why he gave us friends. We need other people with whom we can laugh, cry, work, play, or even be outrageous. Friendships are a blessing, and God uses them to build us up and keep us strong. It is important that we take great care in both having great friends and being great friends. The classic line, "We were never meant to go it alone—even the Lone Ranger had Tonto," is true.

Big Idea

God created friendship and wants us to be wise about it.

Key Texts • Mark 12:28-31

[28]One of the teachers of the law came and heard then debating. Noticing that Jesus had given them a good answer, he asked him, "Of all the commandments, which is the most important?"

[29]"The most important one," answered Jesus, "is this: 'Hear, O Israel, the Lord our God, the Lord is one. [30]Love the Lord your God with all your heart and with all your soul and with all your mind and with all your strength.' [31]The second is this: 'Love your neighbor as yourself.' There is no commandment greater than these."

Mark 2:1-12

A few days later, when Jesus again entered Capernaum, the people heard that he had come home. [2]So many gathered that there was no room left, not even outside the door, and he preached the word to them. [3]Some men came, bringing to him a paralytic, carried by four of them. [4]Since they could not get him to Jesus because of the crowd, they made an opening in the roof above Jesus and, after digging through it, lowered the mat the paralyzed man was lying on. [5]When Jesus saw their faith, he said to the paralytic, "Son, your sins are forgiven."

(continued)

[6]Now some teachers of the law were sitting there, thinking to themselves, [7]"Why does this fellow talk like that? He's blaspheming! Who can forgive sins but God alone?"

[8]Immediately Jesus knew in his spirit that this was what they were thinking in their hearts, and he said to them, "Why are you thinking these things? [9]Which is easier: to say to the paralytic, 'Your sins are forgiven,' or to say, 'Get up, take your mat and walk'? [10]But that you may know that the Son of Man has authority on earth to forgive sins..." He said to the paralytic, [11]"I tell you, get up, take your mat and go home." [12]He got up, took his mat and walked out in full view of them all. This amazed everyone and they praised God, saying, "We have never seen anything like this!"

What You'll Need for This Session

❋ Posterboard and markers (see **Before the Meeting**, point 1)
❋ Copies of **Autograph Hunt** and pens or pencils (page 64)
❋ An overhead projector and a transparency of **Conversation Catalyst** master (page 65)—or enough photocopies for all students (Or else just write it out on your whiteboard or on butcher paper you can post—it's not that long.)
❋ Copies of **Friendship Attitudes** (page 66)

And if you want to do the options...

❋ Video of on-the-street interviews (see **And if you want to do the options...** below, point 2)

Before the Meeting

1. Prepare signs for each of the following words: MAKE, MOVE, MOLD, AND MEND. You'll use your signs to introduce each M word.

And if you want to do the options...

2. Make a video of people on the street describing what they appreciate about their best friends. Or you can interview a kid talking about a friend who is part of your group (see **Video Clip**, page 60).

Introduction

Name That TV Friend

Divide your group into two teams for this trivia quiz on famous pairs of TV and cartoon friends. For each pair of TV friends, invite a member of each team to come forward and name the friend of the character you say. Have the players stand to the right and left of a table, podium, or chair. When players are called, each stands with arms at his or her sides. When you say a character's name, the first player to hit the top of chair (or whatever you're using) gets to give the name of that character's friend. For giving a correct answer, that player's team receives a point. When an incorrect answer is given, the other team gets a chance at the answer.

Fred Flintstone	Barney Rubble
Wilma Flintstone	Betty Rubble
Michael Knight	Kitt
Eddie Haskel	Wally Cleaver
The Skipper	Gilligan
Johnny Quest	Hagi
Gidget	LaRue
Tom	Jerry
Cagney	Lacey
Ren	Stimpy
Laverne	Shirley
Pat Sajak	Vanna White
Barney Fife	Andy Taylor
Popeye	Olive Oil
Mork	Mindy
Ethyl Mertz	Lucy Ricardo
Bullwinkle	Rocky
Yogi	Boo Boo
Laurel	Hardy
Norm	Cliff
Chip	Dale

When you've finished the game, tell the group that you'd now like to tell them about one of your friends. Share an outrageous story of something you did with a friend or group of friends. Go ahead and have fun with it.

Then ask the group to share stories about their friends. The group should be full of stories. Be sure to steer the group away from inappropriate stories. After a bit, stop them. Point out that it's obvious that friends are pretty important to all of us. Tell the group you want to find out what God thinks of friends.

Now read Mark 12:28-31.

Ask your group:

❋ *What is the greatest commandment?* (Love the Lord your God with all your heart and with all your soul and with all your mind and with all your strength.)

❋ *What is the second greatest commandment?* (Love your neighbor as yourself.)

Explain that the second greatest commandment talks about relationships. God is excited about friendships. The rest of the meeting will focus on discovering how we can make our friendships be the best they can be.

Ask your group: *What are some characteristics that describe a great friend?*

Responses may include trustworthiness, understanding, ability to forgive, not holding a grudge, listening, fun to be with, etc.

Option

VIDEO CLIP

Tell your group, "Here's what some people on the street had to say about what they appreciate about their friends." Then show your homemade video.

Say to your group: *Let's look at four words that characterize friendships:* make, move, mold, *and* mend.

MAKE great friends

Refer to your MAKE sign.

Say to your group: *Remember what you were told when you were little?* *"If you want to have a friend, you first must be a friend." This is good advice. We can do this by doing two things: Take initiative and find a common ground with others.*

AUTOGRAPH HUNT

Pass out copies of **Autograph Hunt** (page 64) and pens or pencils. Have the kids mingle and look for people to autograph the appropriate boxes on their sheets.

MOVE to deeper levels of communication

Now refer to your MOVE sign.

Say to your group: *If we want great friendships, we need to talk to and listen to people. Good communication requires moving from surface conversations to deeper ones.*

Next, put the **Conversation Catalyst** transparency (page 65) on the overhead projector (or write the text on your whiteboard). Discuss the example; then have your kids brainstorm other examples of moving a conversation from the surface to a deeper level. Then have them practice those skills through the role plays on the next page.

Invite volunteers to come forward and practice their talking and listening skills in these role play situations:
* Two people waiting in line to buy concert tickets.
* Two new kids who show up at your church youth group.
* A junior higher and an elderly person who are in a doctor's waiting room.
* A telephone conversation between a kid and his or her grandparent.
* Two people on an elevator who haven't yet resolved a conflict between them.

MOLD support in your friendships

Refer to your MOLD sign.

Share this illustration with your group: When we make candles, we pour hot wax into a mold we have created. The mold supports and holds the wax until it has cooled and become firm. Once the wax is hard, it can stand on its own without the support of the mold. If we were to set the candle on a table before the wax had hardened, it would lose its shape, and end up a melted blob. In the same way, we need to support our friends and the needs they have. Without friends, we can wither under life's pressures. When we are struggling or hurting, friends can support us—and we them.

The following games will illustrate your point.

HUMAN PYRAMID

See how high you can build a human pyramid or how many people you can get involved with one pyramid. (Be careful!)

GROUP LAP SIT

Have the entire group stand in a circle. Instruct everyone to turn to the right and shuffle toward the center until they're very close to the people in front of and behind them. On your lead, have the group slowly sit down on each others' laps. The entire group is supporting each other.

Ask your group: What did these two games teach us about the importance of support in friendships?

Scripture Safari

Read Mark 2:1-12 to the group. Then—

Ask your group:
❋ *Who was the friend in need? What was his need?*
❋ *What did his four friends do to meet the need?*
❋ *What do you think their reaction was to the healing?*

Help the group understand that the four friends brought their friend to Jesus because they knew that was where his need would be met. Challenge the group to support their friends by being "stretcher-bearers" and bringing the needs of their friends to Jesus.

The following story appeared in the April 11, 1994, issue of *People* magazine. Share it with your group as a wonderful example of friends supporting friends.

It was a bold and bald-faced—or rather, bald-headed—act of friendship: On March 11, 13 fifth-grade boys lined up to have their pates shaved at the Men's Room, a San Marcos, CA, hair salon. Valuing substance over style, the boys embraced the full-sheared look because their classmate Ian O'Gorman, 11, about to undergo chemotherapy for cancer, would soon lose his hair. Says Ian's pal, Erik Holzhauer, also 11: "You know, Ian's a really nice kid. We shaved our heads because we didn't want him to feel left out."

If compassion were a subject, the Bald Eagles, as the boys now call themselves, would clearly get As. They took notice in early February that Ian was starting to lose weight. Then on February 18 doctors removed a tumor the size of an orange form Ian's small intestine. The diagnosis was non-Hodgkins lymphoma, which has a 68 percent survival rate after five years for children under the age of 15. Two days later, Ian's best friend, Taylor Herber, came to the hospital. "At first I said I would shave my head as a joke, but then I decided to really do it," says Taylor. "I thought it would be less traumatizing for Ian." At school he told the other boys what he was planning, and they jumped on the bandwagon.

"Soon," says Eric, "just about everyone wanted to shave their heads." That included a few girls, who never went through with it, much to Eric's relief—"I don't think Ian wanted to be followed around by a bunch of bald girls"—and Jim Alter, 50, their teacher, who did. "They did all this themselves," he says. "They're just really good kids. It was their own idea. The parents have been very supportive."

Ian, who completes his chemo in May, is already well enough to be playing first base on his Little League baseball team. "What my friends did really makes me feel stronger. It helped me get through all of this," he says gratefully. "I was really amazed that they would do something like this for me." And they won't stop until it's over. "When Ian gets his next CAT scan," vows Erik, "if they decide to do more chemotherapy, we'll shave our heads for another nine weeks."

Way to go, guys!

MEND broken relationships

Say to your group: If anyone has broken friendships, this is the time to heal them. Here's how we can get started:
* *Acknowledge the need for the friendship to be mended. The best place to start is to realize there is a problem and it needs to be corrected. This simple acknowledgment forces us to make a decision.*
* *Pray for God's guidance in the situation. Ask God for direction on how to approach the problem. We need to pray for our friends, that God will work through them, too.*
* *Examine our own hearts. Give ourselves a look-over. Are we part of the problem? Are there areas of our lives that need to be adjusted before we can mend the friendship? Check out Matthew 7:1-5.*
* *Take the first step. Jesus said, "Blessed are the peacemakers." Let's do what peacemakers do by making peace. If we wait for the other person to come to us, nothing may ever happen. Let's go directly to the person without bad-mouthing them to others first.*

Take a moment of silence, inviting kids to tell God about their friendship problems. Suggest that they examine their hearts to find out if they're part of the problem. If so, encourage them to seek their friends' forgiveness.

Conclusion

Friendship Attitudes

Pass out copies of **Friendship Attitudes** (page 66) to everyone in your group. Challenge them to read the verses and match each verse with its correct friendship attitude. Encourage your kids to apply these attitudes in their lives this week.

AUTOGRAPH HUNT

Find someone in the room that matches each of these statements—then have then someone sign inside the corresponding box. Each of the 16 boxes must be signed by a different person—no repeats!

BEEN OUT OF THE COUNTRY	PARENTS OWN A VW
HAS BEEN ON TELEVISION	HAS SNOW SKIED OR WATERSKIED
PLAYS ON A BASKETBALL TEAM	HAS YOUR HAIR COLOR
IS WEARING THE SAME COLOR SHIRT AS YOU	IS SAME HEIGHT AS YOU
LIVES NEAR YOU	HAS THE SAME NUMBER OF LETTERS IN HIS OR HER LAST NAME AS YOU
LIKES BLACK OLIVES ON PIZZA	HAS AN AQUARIUM
HAS SCHOOL ID WITH HIM OR HER	LIVES IN A LARGE FAMILY
WEARS BRACES	PLAYS A MUSICAL INSTRUMENT

CONVERSATION CATALYST

Surface Conversation —>	Sharing Facts —>	Sharing Feelings —>	Deeper Conversation
Hi.	Hi, I'm in your history class at school.	Hi, I'm in your history class at school. I don't like the class very well. How about you?	Hi, I'm in your history class at school. I don't like the class very well. How about you? Would you like to talk about class after school?

FRIENDSHIP ATTITUDES

Read each verse and match it with the appropriate friendship attitude on the right.

Proverbs 17:9   A true friend is honest with the truth.

Proverbs 17:17   One true friend is better than many shallow ones.

Proverbs 18:13   A true friend advises you and cares for you.

Proverbs 18:24   A true friend doesn't gossip about you.

Proverbs 19:7   A true friend stays with you in bad times.

Proverbs 27:6   A true friend really listens to you.

Proverbs 27:9   A true friend likes you for who you are.

Growing Up

Wow, wasn't it just yesterday that we were kids ourselves? Little League baseball and Bobby Sox softball, Barbie dolls and GI Joe, kickball games in the street, dances in the gym, and long conversations on the phone. It's gone by so fast! Let's take a quick return to yesteryear and consider what got us through our own growing-up years. We've learned a lot and have a lot to offer—after all, we *are* called grown-ups.

Big Idea

Believe it or not, grown-ups can tell you a lot about growing up.

Key Text • Jeremiah 29:11

[11]"For I know the plans I have for you," declares the Lord, "plans to prosper you and not to harm you, plans to give you a hope and a future."

What You'll Need for This Session

❋ Some artifacts from your childhood for display (see **Before the Meeting**, point 1)
❋ **Top 10 Bits of Good Advice on Growing Up** signs (pages 75-84), blank sheets of paper, masking tape (and—this is optional—a recording of dramatic music or drum roll; see **Before the Meeting**, point 2)
❋ Baby pictures or slides of students, projector, screen, paper, pencils, and a jar of baby food (see **Before the Meeting**, point 3)
❋ TV, VCR, and a videotape containing interviews of some of your kids' parents (see **Before the Meeting**, point 4)
❋ Cassette or CD *Evolution* by Geoff Moore and the Distance, and cassette/CD player (see **When All is Said and Done**, page 74)

And if you want to do the options...

❋ Adult volunteers to present different bits of advice (see **Option**, page 69)

Before the Meeting

1. Create a display of artifacts from your childhood and teenage years for the kids to look at as they arrive. Include baby albums, old driver's licenses, report cards, prom pictures, trophies, awards, yearbooks, school projects, mementos, etc. Your parents will probably be good sources for some of this stuff. If you can get some slides, put together a slide show, too (see **Yes, I Was a Kid Once, Too**, page 69). Have nothing? Try writing a few tidbits from your growing-up years on separate pieces of paper—where you were born, names of your schools—and spread them around a table. Title the display with something like YES, I WAS A KID ONCE, TOO or A LITTLE HISTORY OF [YOUR NAME].

2. Use the **Top 10 Bits of Good Advice on Growing Up** artwork on pages 75-84 to make 10 signs. Tape them to a front wall or at various places around the room. Then take 10 blank sheets of paper and cover up each sign, numbering the cover sheets with the appropriate Top 10 numbers. When you go through the countdown, you'll remove each cover sheet to reveal the phrase. If you want some drama, have music ready to play as you shout the number, or have kids give a drum roll on the floor. (If you have a large group, use the artwork to create transparencies instead of small signs—that way everyone can read them, regardless of where they're sitting.)

3. Contact some of the parents and ask if you can borrow baby pictures of your students. If you have prints, spread them out on a table. If you have slides, place them in a projector, and set up a screen (see **Baby Picture Guess**, page 70).

4. Interview a few of your kids' parents on video to show for the **Video Clip** on page 70. Ask them to tell funny, off-the-wall stories about when their kids were babies. You can also ask parents a few of the discussion questions in the **Yes, I Was a Kid Once, Too** section on page 69. Be sure to pick kids who won't be devastated by having their parents talk about them on video.

5. Find four individuals to share some thoughts about growing up. We've suggested a parent, you, a senior citizen, and a high school student for the **Personal Advice I-IV** (pages 71-73) sections, but feel free to do what will be most effective for your group.

LEADER HINT

This meeting is built around the **Top 10 Bits of Good Advice on Growing Up** (on the following pages). The advice itself is brief, with the bulk of the program focused on the activities with each Top 10 item. (Some of the activities don't necessarily relate directly to the advice, but they do relate to the general theme.) Develop the program as a personal reflection that you're passing on to the junior highers—a "here's-my-advice-based-on-my-experience" sort of thing.

Insert your name at the beginning of the list—you know, **Darrell's Top 10 Bits of Good Advice on Growing Up.** If you'd

rather compose your own Top 10 words of wisdom, go for it.
Otherwise, this Good Advice should work for most situations.
*There's a lot of advance preparation required for this meeting.
Give yourself enough prep time to pull it off well.*

Introduction

Yes, I Was a Kid Once, Too

Explain that, believe it or not, you were once a junior high student, too. Now that you're grown, you'd like to pass on a few words of wisdom about growing up—so your kids can grow up just like you (tongue in cheek). And now you'd like to present...(your name)'s Top 10 List of Good Advice on Growing Up. Ham it up introducing the list.

If you were able to find some slides, show your slide show and comment as you go. This can be a hoot. If you don't have slides, comment on the artifacts you brought. If you don't have any of those, then point out a few historical facts from your growing-up years (where you were born, who you took to the prom, your first date, etc.).

After you've told a little about yourself, invite the junior highers to tell about their early years. Some questions may include:

❋ *What was the worst thing you ever did?*
❋ *What were you afraid of?*
❋ *What was the weirdest last name of one of your teachers?*
❋ *What was your greatest memory of a babysitter?*
❋ *What was the food that you always refused to eat?*
❋ *What recess game was your favorite?*
❋ *What did you think God looked like?*

Top 10 Bits of Advice on Growing Up

Go ahead and present your list, item by item, beginning with number 10.

Option

Instead of introducing the Top 10 List yourself, invite different adult volunteers to present each topic. Think of adults who have personal stories that speak to particular points. You may even want to eliminate all or a few of the in-between activities, and let the entire evening be "Growing-Up Advice from Wise and Experienced Adults."

10. It gets better.

Begin your dramatic music/drum roll, and reveal your first Top 10 sign.

Say to your group: Life is a process. As the skilled hands of a potter mold and shape the clay, so God is developing us into wonderful creations. All of your days won't be filled with the stress of junior high life. While we will certainly experience frustrations as we grow older, we will also gain new understanding and maturity in how to deal with the stress and frustrations.

Read Philippians 4:6.

BABY PICTURE GUESS

Hand out paper and pencils to the group and show the baby pictures you collected from parents. If you have prints, give everyone a chance to check out the pictures on the table, and record their guesses. (Or you could also have the kids check out the pictures before the meeting and have people guess then.) Be sure to have a leader watch over the pictures so they aren't damaged. If you have slides, show the slides, pausing after each one to give people time to record their guesses. Award a jar of baby food to the kid with the most correct guesses.

9. Work on the inside.

Reveal your second sign, then—

Say to your group: As you grow older, what is on the outside will fade away, but what is on the inside will shine true. The wisest thing you can ever do is work on your inner beauty—what will stand over time, rather than what will fade away.

Read 1 Samuel 16:7.

VIDEO CLIP

Show the video interviews you shot with the parents of kids in your group.

8. Parents know what they're talking about.

Say to your group: Parents have a special ability—they can see the big picture. Why? Because they were once your age. (Amazing, huh?) Now that they're older, they understand what can happen over the long haul. Parents know that if a problem is not dealt with at age 13, it probably will cause problems at age 23. God uses our parents to mold and shape us into something of infinite worth.

Read Proverbs 1:8.

PERSONAL ADVICE I

Invite a parent or two to your meeting to share what they've learned from their own growing-up years.

7. Build up instead of tear down.

Read Galatians 6:7-10.

Say to your group: What we plant (or sow) is what we will harvest (or reap). If we plant wheat seed, we'll harvest wheat. If we plant carrot seed, we'll harvest carrots. If we plant criticism and hurtful words, we'll harvest the same. As you get older, the things you build up or the things you tear down come back to you. You will choose what you'll harvest in the future.

PERSONAL ADVICE II

Share a story from your own life where you reaped either a positive or negative result from your corresponding sowing. Point out what you learned from that experience.

6. Never forget that you can make a difference.

Say to your group: One of the biggest lies going around the country is that junior highers can't do much. They're just occupying time until they get into high school. Baloney! Junior highers are capable, significant, and able to make a radical difference in the world. God believes in you. Don't let anyone tell you otherwise.

Read Jeremiah 29:11.

ADVICE COLUMN

Read the following letter and have your kids discuss the advice they would offer.

Read to your group:
Dear Junior Highers: I have a problem and I don't know what to do. Last week, I walked over to some kids in my class who were talking. When they saw me, they started laughing. They told me that one of the girls had said that I was dumb because I couldn't do the math problem in class. It hurt my feelings. My brother says I'm dumb, too. Don't tell me to talk to my mother; she's too busy with her own problems, and my dad doesn't live with us. —Frustrated Sixth Grader

5. Listen to older people.

Reveal your next sign, then—

Say to your group: Just like parents, older people have the ability to see the big picture. We are foolish to dismiss them and not glean advice from their wisdom. Find a few older people who love the Lord and spend some time with them. Ask them to reflect on their failures and successes. Listen to their passion for God.

Read Psalm 92:12-15.

PERSONAL ADVICE iii

Invite a senior citizen or two to your meeting to offer advice on growing older from their years of wisdom.

4. Set standards.

Say to your group: As you head into maturity, decide to commit yourself to God's principles. Set standards—what you will and won't do—based on what God has given as guidelines. The Bible is your blueprint for future peace.

Read Psalms 119:9-16, 105.
Have your kids discuss the following "reflect on the future" questions.

Ask your group:
❋ *What excites you the most about growing up?*
❋ *What troubles you the most about growing up?*
❋ *Describe yourself at age 17.*
❋ *Describe yourself at age 71.*

3. Failure is normal.

Reveal number three, then—

Say to your group: It's true. Most successful people got that way because they learned through their failures. Failure is part of the growing-up process. If your failures lead to questions, and your questions lead to answers, then failure has done its job. It's also good to remember that God gives us room to fail. He doesn't necessarily love failure, but he loves people who fail, because failure, when properly handled, leads to growth.

Read Proverbs 3:5, 6.

GROWING-UP SCENARIOS

In each of the following scenarios, the characters are adults. As you reflect on the theme of growing up, invite students to come forward and role-play one or more of the scenes. When they're done, ask the group to share their thoughts.

✳ When Christy was in junior high she was always compared to her older sister, Kate. Kate was popular, pretty, and an excellent student. They are now adults and Christy has invited Kate over for coffee. She wants to tell Kate about the struggles she felt growing up in Kate's shadow.

✳ Roger moved from the town where he went to junior high years ago, and now he has returned. He's walking through the halls of the school and reflecting on things he wishes he could change about his junior high years.

✳ On the eve of their son's first day of junior high, Cheryl and Dale sit down and offer words of wisdom based on their own junior high years.

✳ As an adult, Mary Ellen has been invited to speak at the retirement reception of her favorite junior high teacher. She stands up and shares what she's learned over the years and how this teacher inspired her.

✳ Steve, a youth pastor, is writing a book on how to work with junior high kids. He gives his three most important pieces of advice on the subject.

2. Do right.

Say to your group: The greatest compliment you could ever receive is to be called a person of integrity—someone who does right even when others choose to do wrong. Listen to what the Bible says: "I would have you learn this great fact: that a life of doing right is the wisest life there is. If you live that kind of life, you'll not limp or stumble as you run." (Proverbs 4:11-12 Living Bible)

PERSONAL ADVICE IV

Invite a high schooler to your meeting in order to share what he or she has learned about growing up.

1. Jesus is the answer.

Finally reveal your last sign, and—

Say to your group: *The world changes. Jesus doesn't. You can stake everything on that truth. If you want a life that offers things that really matter—hope, joy, peace, love, security—then commit your life to Jesus. Even though your growing-up years will bring all sorts of unexpected changes, Jesus will remain the same. Trust your life with him—he will never let you down.*

Read Hebrews 13:8.

Conclusion

When All Is Said and Done

Play the song "When All Is Said and Done" from the album *Evolution* by Geoff Moore and the Distance (Reunion Records, 1993).

Challenge the group to consider the advice you've offered and to live a life of faithfulness, so that "when all is well and done," they will be proud. When the song has finished, read Psalm 37:23-28. Close in prayer.

10. IT GETS BETTER.

PARENTS KNOW WHAT THEY'RE TALK-ING ABOUT.

BUILD UP INSTEAD OF TEAR TEAR DOWN.

YOU CAN MAKE A DIFFERENCE.

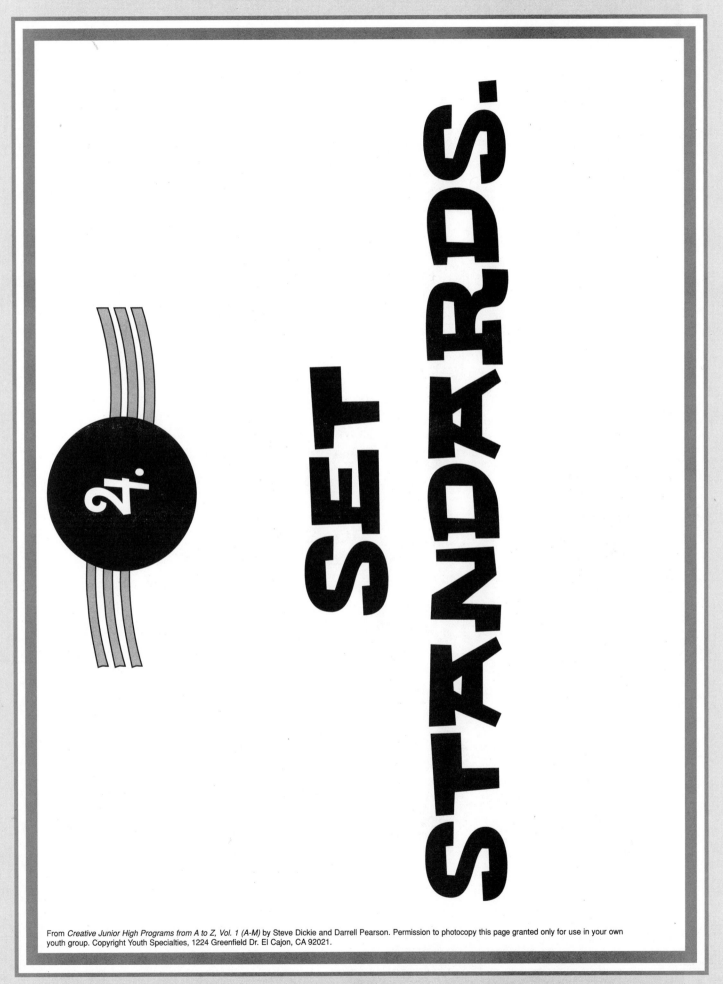

24. SET STANDARDS.

FAILURE IS NORMAL.

"DO RIGHT"

Heroes

We live in a world with few real heroes. When they do come on the scene, they're often not the ones we would want for our students. The irony is that the greatest heroes in the world are often those closest to us, but we don't generally recognize them as heroes—until we take the time to examine the concept of heroism more carefully.

Big Idea

The best heroes in the world are everyday people who do unnoticed and uncommon things for others.

Key Text • Philippians 2:25-30

[25]But I think it is necessary to send back to you Epaphroditus, my brother, fellow worker and fellow soldier, who is also your messenger, whom you sent to take care of my needs. [26]For he longs for all of you and is distressed because you heard he was ill. [27]Indeed he was ill, and almost died. But God had mercy on him, and not on him only but also on me, to spare me sorrow upon sorrow. [28]Therefore I am all the more eager to send him, so that when you see him again you may be glad and I may have less anxiety. [29]Welcome him in the Lord with great joy, and honor men like him, [30]because he almost died for the work of Christ, risking his life to make up for the help you could not give me.

What You'll Need for This Session

❋ Makings for a sub (or gyros, or hero) sandwich and paper towels in a paper bag (see **It May Be Gyros to You…**, pages 86-87)
❋ **Hero Sheet** and pencils (see **Before the Meeting**, point 1)
❋ TV, VCR, and the video *Iron Will* (see **Before the Meeting**, point 2)
❋ A casette or CD of a contemporary piano piece and a cassette/CD player, a Band-Aid, a flower, car keys, and a shawl (see **Mom Mime**, page 88)

Before the Meeting

1. Prepare your **Hero Sheet** by cutting out pictures of famous people from newspapers and magazines and gluing them to a sheet of paper. Choose people who are considered heroic—national leaders, Mother Theresa, local award winners, sports stars, etc. Make copies for everyone.

2. Cue the video *Iron Will* to the scene where the father cuts the rope to save his son—but loses his own life (see **Video Clip**, page 87).

3. Find two students to act out the **Mom Mime** on page 88. The mime is simple to learn, rehearse, and perform. It involves one male and one female who play changing roles throughout each scene. A contemporary piano piece works well as background music during the mime.

4. Ask a willing student ahead of time to close in prayer. Ask him or her to pray that the group would all recognize the everyday people doing things for them, and in turn be great "heroes" to others.

Introduction

Rock, Scissors, Paper: Team-Style

This game is based on the classic game "Rock, Scissors, Paper." In the game, two people face each other, count one, two, three, and then show a hand motion that represents one of the three objects. The rock is a tight fist; paper is a flat hand; scissors is the index and middle finger held like a pair of scissors. As you probably know, rock smashes scissors, scissors cut paper, paper covers rock.

For this version of the game, split your group into two teams, separating them with a center line in the middle of the room. Each team should face the other, in as long a line as the room permits. Each team chooses a "hero" to lead the team. Each hero first meets with his or her group at the far end of their side of the room. The hero chooses either rock, scissors, or paper for the entire team. Once chosen, the two teams meet back at the center line. After you count one-two-three, everyone shows their hands. The winning team chases the other team to their back wall, trying to tag as many opposing team members as they can. Anyone tagged before reaching the wall becomes a member of the winning team. If the two teams have chosen the same object, both retreat to the wall for new instructions from their "heroes." When the game is done, sit everyone down on the floor to rest.

Group Discussion

It May Be Gyros to You, But It's Hero to Us

Start off this section by walking out with a paper bag that contains a few paper towels and the ingredients for the sub sandwich. For the purposes of this lesson, we'll call it a "hero" sandwich (despite the fact that *hero* is a corruption of the Greek word for this sandwich, *gyros*). Talk about how good the sandwich is going to be, how hungry you are, how you can't wait to sink your teeth into it. Refer casually to the sandwich as a "hero." (If this isn't a common term for a sub sandwich where you live, tell the students that *hero* is what it's called in Los Angeles or Washington, D.C., or Dallas, or whatever part of the country is exotic to your students.)

Set out your paper towels and begin building your sandwich. Explain all the ingredients you're putting in, and why each is important. Top off the sandwich with your favorite condiment. It may be the smallest addition, tell them, but it's the most important.

Start eating the sandwich. Take your time chewing; the pauses between your bites while you chew should be long and, to the kids, a little awkward.

Say to your group: *I suppose you're all wondering why I'm eating a sandwich and you're not. **[long pause for another bite and chewing]** That's a good question. **[another bite and pause]** You probably wish that I'd share the sandwich with all of you. **[another bite and pause]** In fact, I'll bet I'd be a pretty big hero myself if I brought in a sandwich for everybody! **[another bite and pause]** Well, I don't have any sandwiches. **[If you have a small group of kids, go ahead and split up the hero for everybody]** Big let-down, huh? But, I do have some other heroes—and I have enough of* <u>those</u> *to go around.*

Now pass out your **Hero Sheets** and pencils.

Say to your group: *I want you to take a look at these people. Which ones do you think are heroes? Why? Are some more heroic than others? Circle your favorites and write next to their pictures just what it is that makes them a hero.*

Give them two minutes for this. Then have them divide into groups of three to five people (if possible, have an adult volunteer lead each small group), and—

Say to your group: *Take about five minutes to tell the other people in your group who you chose and why.*

Video Clip

Show the five-minute clip from the video *Iron Will*. When the clip is over, have a student ready to read the Scripture passage (see **Scripture Safari**) before the groans begin that the video is over!

Scripture Safari

Have your kids read Philippians 2:25-30—the story of Epaphroditus and his sacrifice for the Philippians.

Ask your group:
* *What did Ep (use the short form) do for everyone else?*
* *What do you think the specific action he took was?*

Get Personal

Ask students to make quick groups of three and four. Have each person tell the others in his or her group the one person in the world who has influenced him or her the most—in other words, the Epaphroditus in his or her life. What has this person done? Why has that been so influential? Give each student two minutes to share.

Next—

Discuss the following questions:

❋ *Have you ever done anything to recognize what this person has done for you?*
❋ *Have you ever been an "Ep" to someone else? Who? What have you done?*
❋ *Did you receive any thanks for doing this?*
❋ *Why is it that we often forget to recognize those who've done the most for us?*

Mom Mime

The scenes:

1. The guy plays a little boy who has just scraped his arm. He runs crying to Mom, who kisses his arm, puts a Band-Aid on the scrape, and then sends him on his way. As he walks away, she looks at the audience and mouths, "That's my boy."

2. The son (older now) is playing in a basketball game. Mom sits in a chair and cheers wildly. After passing the ball to imaginary players, the son shoots the winning basket. Mom once again mouths to someone near her, "That's my boy."

3. Mom and son are arguing about something. It's a serious argument. Make sure the audience picks up on the intensity. After a few seconds, Mom holds out her hand, palm facing up. The son takes keys from his pocket and tosses them high in the air for her to catch. Mom slowly mouths the phrase "That's my boy" to herself.

4. Son takes flower and holds it where a suit coat chest pocket would be, and walks off. He returns and he's beaming. It's his wedding day, and he walks to center and faces audience. Mom has back to audience as if she is sitting in a pew facing him. The son mimes taking the arm of his bride, turning to a minister, putting a ring on the bride, pulling back a veil, kissing his bride, and strutting down the aisle. He smiles at Mom as he passes, then she mouths the same phrase again.

5. Son returns down center aisle, this time he's grieving. He's carrying the flower in one hand. Mom picks up shawl and uses it to dry her tears. The two

embrace, then turn and look at the ground. Son slowly tosses flower on the ground.

6. Mom sits in the center facing audience. Shawl is over her head and she should mime holding a remote and watching TV. She is now obviously old. Son knocks on door, enters, the two talk and smile, son looks at watch, apologizes, and leaves. Mom returns to TV. Son pauses, turns, re-enters room, then slowly embraces her. Mom looks surprised. He mouths "Thanks, Mom," looks at the audience and mouths, "That's my mom." They embrace again and freeze. Music fades.

Conclusion

Just Pray

Really, that's all. A simple prayer is a fitting conclusion to this session.

Integrity

Standing up for what is right, even though others choose to do wrong, is called integrity. Integrity is the mark of someone who takes his or her faith seriously. As we commit our lives to Jesus, he challenges us not only to believe in him, but also to live out our faith with the passion it deserves. In the face of a disbelieving world, passionate Christians stand for God's way. They stand for integrity.

Big Idea

God has called us to stand for his way, not the world's way.

Key Text • Philippians 4:8

[8]Finally, brothers, whatever is true, whatever is noble, whatever is right, whatever is pure, whatever is lovely, whatever is admirable—if anything is excellent or praiseworthy—think about such things.

What You'll Need for This Session

❀ Plastic trash can (see **Superman Trivia**, page 92)
❀ Sheets of paper and pencils (see **Acronym Definition**, page 93)
❀ Copies of **The Game of Integrity Game Sheet**, sets of **The Game of Integrity Game Cards**, paper in assorted colors (see **Before the Meeting**, point 1), and a coin (see **The Game of Integrity**, page 96)
❀ Eight sheets of paper and markers (see **Before the Meeting**, point 2)

And if you want to do the options...

❀ Newsprint, posterboard, or paper; markers and masking tape (see **Before the Meeting**, page 92, point 3)

Before the Meeting

1. Make copies of **The Game of Integrity Game Sheet** and a set of **Game Cards** for each game sheet (pages 98-99). You'll need one game sheet for every two to three kids. Make small game-sheet markers for each student by cutting out 1/2-inch squares from different colored paper.

2. Take eight sheets of paper and, in bold letters, write one of the following words on each sheet: TRUE, NOBLE, RIGHT, PURE, LOVELY, ADMIRABLE, EXCELLENT, PRAISEWORTHY. Put a piece of rolled-up masking tape on the back of each one (see **Think about These Things**, page 97).

And if you want to do the options...

3. Write Proverbs 4:11 in the *Living Bible* version (see **Proverbs on High**, page 97) on newsprint, posterboard, or paper so it's large enough to be seen when taped to the ceiling. Here it is:

> I would have you learn this one great fact: that a life of doing right is the wisest life there is.

Introduction

Superman Trivia

Divide your group into teams and give them designated areas in which to sit. In one central location, place a plastic trash can. When you read a Superman trivia question, if someone knows the answer, he or she jumps up and tags the trash can. The first person to tag the can gets to answer the question. If you have large teams, designate a representative for each team to tag the can when the team has an answer. This prevents a horde of kids rushing the trash can.

1. Who was Superman's father? (Jor-El)
2. Where did Superman go to high school? (Smallville High)
3. Who was Superman's high school girlfriend? (Lana Lang)
4. Who played Superman in the 1950 TV show? (George Reeves)
5. Who played Superman in the movies? (Christopher Reeve)
6. What can't Superman see through? (lead)
7. What is Superman's alias? (Clark Kent)
8. Where does Clark Kent work? (*The Daily Planet* newspaper)
9. Who is Clark Kent's boss? (Perry White)
10. What element can hurt Superman? (kryptonite)
11. What is Superman's polar getaway? (Fortress of Solitude)
12. Who is the female reporter at the *Daily Planet*? (Lois Lane)
13. Where was Superman born? (the planet Krypton)
14. Superman is faster than what? (a speeding bullet)
15. Superman is more powerful than what? (a locomotive)

At the conclusion of the game, tell your group that Superman was famous for standing up for what was right. You know, the old "truth, justice, and the American way" thing. That commitment to do right, even when there's the option to do wrong, has a name. It's called *integrity*.

Understanding Integrity

Explain to the group that integrity is a mark of the Christian faith. James 1:22 challenges us, "Do not merely listen to the word, and so deceive yourselves. Do what it says." When we take our faith seriously, we must take action. That means standing up for right, even when others are choosing to do wrong.

Explain to the group that integrity means standing up for what's right in two ways: first, in the big things, when everyone can see your decision; second, in the little things, when no one else ever knows. Share some of the following examples with your kids (add other examples if you wish).

Say to your group: Here are some big things that everyone notices:
❋ *Saying no to alcohol or drugs at a party.*
❋ *Sticking up for someone when everyone else is picking on them.*
❋ *Walking away from a group that is telling crude jokes.*
❋ *Giving up your seat on a crowded bus to an elderly person.*

In the little things, when no one would ever know:

❋ *Not cheating on a take-home exam.*
❋ *Refusing to watch an inappropriate TV show when alone.*
❋ *Praying for someone who has done you wrong.*
❋ *Returning correct change when undercharged at a store.*

Now ask your group:

❋ *What are some other examples of integrity?*
❋ *Why is it important to have integrity when everyone can see your actions?*
❋ *Why is it important to have integrity when no one can see your actions?*

ACRONYM DEFINITION

Divide your group into small groups. Give each group a sheet of paper and a pencil, then have them define integrity by creating an acronym—coming up with a word or phrase for each letter of the word. Here's an example:

Intense about integrity
Never compromise truth
Totally committed to honesty
Eager to do what's right
God's way above all
Righteousness rules
Ignores peer pressure
True to God's word
You can do it!

Acknowledging Integrity

Ask your group: Can you think of a classic example from literature, television, or the movies where a character demonstrated integrity?

Have them share their answers.

Next, read the following real-life story from the March 20, 1994, *Los Angeles Times* of one man's commitment to integrity.

At 5:15 on a chilly summer morning in 1940, Chiune Sugihara awoke to the sound of a low rumble outside. He was no industrialist, like the German who saved more than 1,000 Jews by employing them in his factories, a story captured in the movie *Schindler's List*.

Rather, Sugihara was Japan's consul general in Lithuania.

On this particular morning, he peeked outside the curtained windows of the consular building and was startled to see the quiet street choked with a crowd of more than 200.

Unnerved and afraid, Sugihara woke his wife and three children and hid them in a closet. But when he took a closer look, he saw that the people outside were not hostile. They were desperate.

Their eyes were bloodshot. They looked fatigued. There were older men in beards and hats, young boys, mothers holding infants. When they saw him, some put their palms together in prayerful entreaty. Others, excited, tried to climb over the fence.

They were Polish Jews fleeing the encroaching German army, and Sugihara was their last hope to avoid the Nazi death camps.

As war rumbled through Europe, all escape routes from Poland had been cut off except a treacherous journey through the frozen hinterlands of the Soviet Union via Lithuania. From the eastern port of Vladivostok, the refugees could sail to Japan and, from there, try to flee to China, North America, or the Dutch colony of Curacao. But they needed a transit visa through Japan. So they lined the streets, waiting for days, outside the Japanese mission.

The pleas presented Sugihara with the kind of searing dilemma that confronts few people in a lifetime: a choice between individual conscience and national duty, between life and death. To issue the visas, he would have to defy orders from his government not to accommodate the Jews.

Three times the 40-year-old official sent urgent cables to the Japanese government seeking permission to proceed; three times he was refused. Japan was on the verge of entering a military alliance with Germany and Italy and was being pressured to cooperate in addressing "the Jewish problem."

"I had to do something," Sugihara told the U.S. military newspaper *Stars and Stripes* a year before his death at age 86 in 1986. "Those people told me the kind of horror they would have to face if they didn't get away from the Nazis, and I believed them. There was no place for them to go. I had to look at it from the standpoint of humanity. I could only be fired and returned to Japan. What else were they going to do?"

He decided to defy his government, a choice that would change his life forever. For 28 days, from July 31, 1940, until the Japanese government ordered him out of Lithuania to Berlin, the consul general feverishly handwrote transit visas. From morning to night, he interviewed one applicant after another and wrote one visa after another.

Sugihara kept writing permits even after he closed the consulate and moved to a hotel for a few days to wait for the train that would take him and his family to Germany. He kept writing even on the train, thrusting the precious pieces of paper through the window to waiting hands outside.

In the end, he managed to write an estimated 1,600 visas, which the Israeli government and various scholars credit with saving the lives of 2,000 to 6,000 Jews. (An entire family could travel on one visa.)

Ask your group:
※ *What is a real-life example of integrity that you have seen?*
※ *What are real-life examples of integrity found in the Bible?*

Integrity in the Bible

Check out these classic examples of integrity—three from the book of Daniel and one from Genesis. After reading each story, then—

Ask your group:
※ *What was the example of integrity?*
※ *Why do you think the people did what they did?*
※ *Was there a cost in their decision?*

1. Daniel 3:1-30. **Shadrach, Meshach,** and **Abednego** refused to bow to the king's idol, even though they knew it would mean death in a furnace. They stood for right—for all to see.

2. Daniel 1:1-21. **Daniel** resolved to live according to his conviction about his physical diet. In what seemed like such a small thing (who would really care if he ate the king's food?), Daniel chose to do what was right.

3. Daniel 6:1-28. **Daniel** continued to pray despite the king's decree that no one would pray except to him. Daniel honored his commitment to God even though it meant being thrown into a lion's den.

4. Genesis 39:1-23. His boss's wife simply wanted to seduce **Joseph**, and she kept making passes at him. When Joseph could no longer avoid her advances, he literally ran away from her, standing true to what was right before God.

When you're finished with the discussion, it's time to play **The Game of Integrity**.

THE GAME OF INTEGRITY

Hand out copies of The Game of Integrity Game Sheet (page 98), Game Cards (page 99), game sheet markers, and a coin. Have two to three people per game sheet. To move game pieces, players flip the coin—heads, one space; tails, two spaces.

When your students have finished playing, ask them, "What did you learn about integrity by playing the game? What were the hardest decisions that you had to make?"

Making Decisions for Integrity

Now divide into small groups, or discuss as a whole, these integrity-threatening situations. After each story, then—

Ask your group: What would you do? What should you do?

Explain to the group that the goal of integrity is to make what we *should* do what we *would* do.

❋ Carla is a teacher's aide for English class. The teacher has entrusted her with taking attendance each day as soon as class begins. Before class, a guy Carla has been wanting to date asks her to mark him present even though he's planning to cut class. He quickly walks away before Carla can give an answer.

❋ Some of your friends invite you to go with them to the movies tonight. It sounds like you will have a good time if you go. When you arrive at the movies, you realize that your friends have decided to sneak into the theater through a side door. You have to think quickly. Should you sneak in with your friends, pay for your ticket, but still sit with your friends even though they didn't pay, or turn around and walk home?

✳ It's happened again. Your math teacher has left the room while the class works on an assignment. Meanwhile, the grade book is being passed around the class. Since the teacher enters homework, quiz, and test grades in pencil, it's a snap to change them. The grade book is getting close to you. Should you take it and change a few grades? Should you let it pass? Should you keep your mouth shut or tell the teacher?

Option

PROVERBS ON HIGH

Take the Proverbs 4:11 sign you made earlier and tape it to the ceiling. Have everyone lay on their backs and read the verse.

Conclusion

Think about These Things

Say to your group: God has given us guidance on how to live a life of integrity. The challenge of Philippians 4:8 becomes a yardstick by which to measure our decisions: "Whatever is true, whatever is noble, whatever is right, whatever is pure, whatever is lovely, whatever is admirable—if anything is excellent or praiseworthy—think about such things."

As you read the verse aloud, take the eight sheets you prepared earlier, and tape up each word as it's read.

Ask the group to think about areas of their lives where they might not be standing for integrity. Ask them to consider Philippians 4:8 and how it might relate to these areas.

Close with silent prayer.

THE GAME OF INTEGRITY

Pick a Card

If you have been a person of integrity this week. Go ahead one space.

Pick a Card

Read Proverbs 29:7 How does integrity speak to those who are poor?

Pick a Card

Read Proverbs 13:3 Why is gossip not the way of integrity?

Read Proverbs 11:20 How would you say this verse in your own words?

Pick a Card

Pick a Card

Read Proverbs 11:1 Why is cheating not the way of integrity?

Read Proverbs 12:22 Why is lying not the way of integrity?

PLACE CARDS HERE

Pick a Card

Pick a Card

Read Proverbs 10:9 Why does integrity bring security?

I would have you learn this one great fact: that a life of doing right is the wisest life there is. If you live that kind of life, you'll not limp or stumble as you run.

Proverbs 4:11-12
(Living Bible)

Read Proverbs 21:29 What is the difference between a wicked and an upright person?

Pick a Card

START

FINISH

Pick a Card

FLIP A COIN. HEADS MOVE ONE SPACE, TAILS MOVE TWO.

The Game of Integrity
Game Cards

Your older brother comes to a red light late at night. No one is around. What would you do? What should you do?

Through an error, you receive a paid-cable TV channel for free. What would you do? What should you do?

The postman leaves a cool magazine at your house by mistake. It belongs to someone on another street. What would you do? What should you do?

Your friend gossips to you about someone you dislike. What would you do? What should you do?

You're given too much change at the store. It's only 15 cents. What would you do? What should you do?

Your friends want you to tape copies of your music cassettes for them. You have heard that it is illegal. What would you do? What should you do?

You didn't do a reading assignment. The teacher passes around a paper asking everyone to sign the paper to indicate if they have done the reading or not. What would you do? What should you do?

Your coach tells you to do something that's against the rules to win a game. What would you do? What should you do?

A very popular kid in your class is picking on someone. What would you do? What should you do?

While spending the night at a friend's house, everyone decides to watch pornographic movies on late-night cable TV. What would you do? What should you do?

Your best friend's steady tells you that he or she actually likes you. What would you do? What should you do?

You borrow a pen at school and forget to return it. What would you do? What should you do?

judging

The capacity for criticizing and judging others unfairly is a talent that reaches its full potential, unfortunately, in middle school. Junior high students have an unlimited capacity to attack others while overlooking their own inadequacies. Jesus brought attention to the problem of judging in the Sermon on the Mount when he discussed the "log in your own eye" concept, and that's the focus of this session.

Big Idea

The only person worth trying to change is yourself.

Key Texts • Matthew 7:1-5; 18:23-35

"Do not judge, or you too will be judged. [2]For in the same way you judge others, you will be judged, and with the measure you use, it will be measured to you.

[3]"Why do you look at the speck of sawdust in your brother's eye and pay no attention to the plank in your own eye? [4]How can you say to your brother, 'Let me take the speck out of your eye,' when all the time there is a plank in your own eye? [5]You hypocrite, first take the plank our of your own eye, and then you will see clearly to remove the speck from your brother's eye."

What You'll Need for This Session

❋ Custodian or reasonable facsimile of one (see **Before the Meeting**, point 1)
❋ Large log (or cardboard log used to roll carpet on), mattresses, and pillows (see **Log-Rolling**, page 103)
❋ TV, VCR, and your two self-produced videos (see **Before the Meeting**, point 2)
❋ Copies of the **Spontaneous Melodrama** (pages 104-105) for each actor

Before the Meeting

1. The person you chose as your custodian needs to be easy going enough to play along with his or her role in the program (see **A Custodial Chewing Out**, below; **Video Clips**, page 105; and **Custodial Sermon**, page 106).

2. You'll need to make two videos (see **Video Clips**, page 105). Video 1 is supposedly a clip of the custodian's house (of course, any house will do). Make sure a few things are out of place—socks on the floor, magazines lying around, etc. In reality, the house will be fairly clean, but you'll talk about it as if it's the end of the world. Video 2 needs to be on a different tape. It will be a short video of the local dump, an auto wrecking yard, or a salvage yard—anywhere really disgusting. This will supposedly be your house.

3. Think about who you'll use in the **Spontaneous Melodrama** (pages 104-105). You'll need eight people.

Introduction

A Custodial Chewing Out

Say to your group: Before we get started tonight, we have a special guest with us who has an important announcement to make. Say hello to our church custodian.

The custodian then explains that he or she is there because of an ongoing problem at church: namely, the mess the junior high group leaves in their room each week. The custodian concludes by pleading with the students to take care of their room like the young married class does, or the Ambassadors or the Bereans or the Thirtysomethings (the custodian should use class names of actual groups at your church). After he or she leaves—

Say to your group: Can you believe that? They think we're the worst in the church? But has anyone seen the cake crumbs all over the Fellowship Hall carpet after a wedding reception?

Ad-lib your frustration, and mention that you have a plan to teach the church a lesson. Segue to the following game.

LOG-ROLLING

To play, you'll need a large round log (or a cardboard log like they use to roll carpet on). Make a big deal as you bring in the big log—have several students or leaders carry it in as if it's a statue or an idol.

Lay the log down on the floor, with mattresses on either side of it. Next, have kids take turns trying to knock each other off the log. To do this, have students stand at each end of the log, doing their best to balance. Let them whack each other with pillows to knock each other off the log. If balance is too big a problem, have a leader hold the log while they battle. Make sure everyone gets a chance to try it, and then see who's the best.

Small Talk

Explain to your group: Wood is mentioned a lot in the Bible. Everyone knows about Noah and the ark, and it was, of course, two pieces of wood that made up the cross on which Jesus died. One of the most interesting mentions of wood was when Jesus talked about getting a log stuck in your eye. Listen to this.
Read Matthew 7:1-5.

Ask your group: Has anyone ever had a log the size of this one stuck in your face? Probably not, but I'll bet you've had some painful things stuck in your eye. Who's got a story about a time you got something in your eye?

Someone is sure to have a gory story to tell. After several stories, emphasize how painful it is to have something in your eye. Ask for a volunteer to come up and you'll shove the log into his or her eye. After nobody volunteers, talk about how painful that would be, much less possible.

Ask your group: So what do you think Jesus was trying to teach through this story?

Let one or two students talk about the meaning of Jesus' message (which is not to judge others when your own faults are much bigger). To illustrate this concept, pick eight volunteers to perform the "spontaneous melodrama" that begins on the next page.

Spontaneous Melodrama

In this melodrama each student plays his or her role by acting out—melodramatically!—whatever you say. Encourage audience participation, too. The script is based on Matthew 18:23-25. You'll need eight students to play the following roles:

* Unmerciful servant (female)
* Servant's wife (male)
* King
* Throne (two students)
* Pity
* Servant's friend
* Jailer

As the scene opens...Onstage are the Throne (center), the Jailer, and Pity. Offstage are the King, Servant, Servant's wife, and Servant's friend.

Therefore, the kingdom of heaven is like a king *(walks onstage, sits on throne—get the audience to cheer)* who wanted to settle accounts with his servants. A man was brought to him who owed him a million dollars. *(Servant enters with his wife—get audience to boo)* Since he was not able to pay the debt, the king ordered that he and his wife be thrown into prison. *(Jailer starts throwing Servant and his wife around)* The servant fell on his knees before the king...*(to Jailer:)* the king's knees. *(Jailers should fall on the King's knees)*

"Have pity on me!" the servant cried. So the king threw pity all over the servant *(King throws Pity on the servant)*—and on his wife. Then the king forgave the servant's debt and let him go *(audience cheers for King)*.

On his way out, the servant ran into an old friend who owed him five bucks. The servant grabbed him and began to chock his friend. The servant's wife began to choke her husband. The servant said to his friend, "Pay me back what you owe me!" The friend fell on his knees...*(to Servant's friend)* the servant's knees...and begged for pity. But the servant refused. Instead, he had the jailer throw the man into prison. Then he had the jailer throw his wife into prison.

When the king found out, he began to scream in anger. He jumped up and down in anger. He began doing the twist—in anger. He called the servant in.

"You wicked servant!" he said. "I cancelled your debt because you begged me to. Shouldn't you have mercy on your friend as well? Jailer, take this ungrateful servant away and torture him."

So the jailer tortured him by tickling him, then by slapping him silly. As the ultimate torture, the jailer sang a romantic rendition of "I'm Dreaming of a White Christmas."

Then the king said, "This is how the heavenly father will treat each of you unless you forgive your sister and brother from your heart."

End

Ask for a student volunteer to talk about a time he or she accused someone else of a problem that he or she too had been guilty of (sibling stories are easy here). To wrap up the story—

Ask your group: Why are we so quick to accuse others?

Video Clips

Remind the students about how the custodian nailed them for making the church so dirty. Tell them that you secretly filmed the custodian's home, and found some shocking things. Show Video 1. Narrate the video as if you're looking at the custodian's home, exaggerating the mess. When the video is done—

Say to your group: Can you believe it? And he has the nerve to criticize us!

Just then, have the custodian reappear, holding Video 2, and announce that he or she filmed *your* house—and it was even *more* shocking. Show Video 2 (with shots of the dump, auto wreck yard, etc). When it's done, confess to the group that even you can be guilty of the log-in-your-eye principle.

Conclusion

Custodial Sermon: The Janitor on Judging

Let the custodian wrap it up with a short devotional he or she prepared beforehand. It's best if he can prepare this himself—but just in case, here's at least a brief outline you can give the custodian to prime the pump.

✳ **Hook:** The introduction—a personal story of a time you judged someone else unfairly. Who was it? What happened? How did you feel?

* **Book:** Read Matthew 7:1-5 in a very different translation from the one the students would be accustomed to hearing—maybe *The New Testament in Modern English* by J.B. Phillips, or *The Message* by Eugene Peterson.
* **Look:** Explain what this verse means to you in short, simple terms.
* **Took:** Give the students a practical suggestion for applying this principle. For example, you might say, "Tomorrow, when you're all set to criticize your lab partner for that irritating habit she has, think for a moment about what Jesus said. Anything about yourself that could use as much attention—or correction—as whatever it is about your lab partner that bugs you?

Close the meeting with a prayer.

Know-it-alls

There are few things more frustrating than a know-it-all—someone who has all the answers. Junior highers wish they could find some way to stop know-it-alls from providing the answers. In this meeting you'll set kids up a little. They will think all along that they're going to do something about these people, only to find out at the end that the focus is on doing something about themselves.

Big Idea

The only know-it-all you can change is yourself.

Key Text • Genesis 37:3-8

³Now Israel loved Joseph more than any of his others sons, because he had been born to him in his old age; and he made a richly ornamented robe for him. ⁴When his brothers saw that their father loved him more than any of them, they hated him and could not speak a kind word to him.

⁵Joseph had a dream, and when he told it to his brothers, they hated him all the more. ⁶He said to them, "Listen to this dream I had: ⁷We were binding sheaves of grain out in the field when suddenly my sheaf rose and stood upright, while your sheaves gathered around mine and bowed down to it."

⁸His brothers said to him, "Do you intend to reign over us? Will you actually rule us?" And they hated him all the more because of his dream and what he had said.

What You'll Need for This Session

❋ Scotch tape (see **The Unrelenting Interrupter**, page 108)
❋ Transparency of **Teen Jeopardy Gameboard** (page 113), an overhead projector, and blank paper squares OR a whiteboard, markers, index cards, masking tape, and 3 copies of **Teen Jeopardy—The Sketch** (pages 109-112; see **Before the Meeting**, point 1)

❊ *Horton Hears a Who* by Dr. Seuss, a rocking chair, and a lamp (see **Story Time**, page 114)

And if you want to do the options...

❊ Your own version of the **Teen Jeopardy Gameboard** (see **Before the Meeting**, below)

Before the Meeting

1. **Teen Jeopardy—The Sketch** (page 109-112) requires some preparation and rehearsal beforehand. It involves two contestants: one, a typical-looking teenager who will answer every question wrong (but the game-show host will always say he's right). Dr. Telligence should be some authority figure such as a teacher, parent, college professor, or someone who supposedly knows everything about everything. There is also the game-show host, Albert Dweebek, who should be a leader skilled at skits and humor, and an assistant to help with the gameboard.

Make an overhead transparency of the **Teen Jeopardy Gameboard** (page 113). Cut out squares of blank paper and lay them over the boxes on the gameboard transparency. The squares will be removed by the assistant at the appropriate times during the sketch.

If you cannot obtain an overhead projector, draw the game board on a whiteboard with markers and tape index cards labeled with the dollar amounts over the appropriate boxes.

And if you want to do the options...

2. If you choose to play **Teen Jeopardy—The Game** (page 114), make up your own categories and have another game board prepared the same way as in the sketch. Make sure one of the categories is Bible Trivia, and at least one other is really tough.

Introduction

The Unrelenting Interrupter

Begin the program by having an adult leader welcome everyone and give an overview of the night, plus a summary of upcoming events, etc. During this talk, another leader should keep gently interrupting to correct the first one. The tone of these interruptions should be gentle and not overwhelming (not "You don't know anything!" but, "Isn't the time for that meeting 7, not 7:30?...") The first leader should be increasingly frustrated with all these suggestions.

So the opening could sound something like this (of course, ad-lib as much as you want). Of course, replace the two leaders' names with names of actual leader-actors:

Kathy: Welcome to youth group tonight. We're going to have a great time, play some games, and talk about how to deal with other people.

Lynn: (*seated*) Actually, Kathy, it's not exactly just other people, but a certain type of person who is the most frustrating to us.

Kathy: Uh-h, that's true, but I wanted to keep it kind of general so no one would figure out everything we're going to do before we start.

Lynn: That's nice, but isn't accuracy better? Isn't it best to let these kids know as precisely as possible what we're doing tonight?

Kathy: Okay, great. I'll think about that (*turns attention back to group*). Well, I hope you've had a great week; it's been a tough one here in our city, hasn't it? Can you believe all this rain? Maybe some of your houses have been flooded or you've had some problems with all this rain.

Lynn: You know, Kathy, the spring actually has been very dry; we need all this water. It's really a godsend, even if it created a few problems.

Kathy: Great. As I was saying before, it's been a tough week. But that's why it's sure good to come together and spend a little time thinking about what God has to say about our lives. He's ready to help us.

Lynn: Kathy...

Kathy: What!?

Lynn: Well, doesn't that create a minor theological question that we can't really deliver on?

Kathy: I've had it. Come up here. *(She takes out a roll of Scotch tape and, finally fed up with Lynn the know-it-all, tapes up her face. In her frustration Kathy creates quite an artistic creation, pulling Lynn's facial skin in all sorts of directions—and taping it in place)* There! I've *always* wanted to do that to somebody else. Wouldn't it be wonderful if we could just shut up know-it-alls once and for all? Speaking of know-it-alls, we have several with us tonight. Let's play "Teen Jeopardy"!

Teen Jeopardy-The Sketch

The game begins by introducing the game-show host, Albert Dweebek. Have everyone hum the "Jeopardy" theme song, then have Albert host the show as follows. The script begins on page 110.

Teen Jeopardy—The Sketch

Characters:
> **Albert Dweebek,** the emcee
> **Sue** (use this student actor's actual name throughout the sketch
> instead of "Sue")
> **Dr. Ian Telligence**

Setting:
> A "Jeopardy"-type game show

Albert: Welcome to **"Teen Jeopardy,"** the show where teenagers finally get to turn the tables on those know-it-all adults. Let's welcome our contestants. First, our defending champion—he's in the eighth grade for the eighth consecutive year at Washington Middle School—would you welcome Sue!

Sue: Thanks, Albert, I'm ready to win a few more thousand dollars.

Albert: I'm sure you will. Let's meet the challenger. He's a professor of microbiology—whatever that is—at our local university; holds three doctoral degrees—whatever those are—and he's memorized large portions of the Chicago phone book—would you welcome Doctor Ian Telligence!

Dr. Telligence: (*looks nervous*) Thank you, Albert. I'm ready to play.

Albert: Well, we wish you all the luck (*smirks at audience*). Here are our categories! (*The assistant should be ready to pull squares off the transparency or cards off the whiteboard, revealing the "answers" underneath.*) The first-round categories are: American History, Geography, and Language. Let's play! Sue, you get to go first.

Sue: Thanks Albert. I'll take American History for 100. (*Here the assistant removes the card and Albert reads the "question in the form of an answer."*)

Albert: A year when America was involved in a terrible civil war.

Dr. T: (*pretends to pound button*) What is 1865?

Albert: Oh, I'm sorry, that's wrong. Sue?

Sue: What is 1492?

Albert: That's correct!

Sue: American History for 200.

Dr. T: Excuse me, Albert, but that's not the correct answer.

Albert: Right. Here we go. The year that man first walked on the moon's surface.

Dr. T: (*punching button*) What is 1969?

Albert: Sorry, that's wrong. Sue?

Sue: What is 1492?

Albert: That's correct!

Dr. T: (*throwing a fit*) That's not even close! I happen to know that the precise date of the moon landing was on—

Albert: Zip it up, Doctor. Sue?

Sue: History for 300.

Albert: You're on a roll! The year that the Pilgrims landed at Plymouth Rock.

(*Doctor T. doesn't hit the button—he's too frustrated*)

Sue: (*hitting button*) Tough one, Albert. What is 1492?

Albert: Right again! Make it a grand slam.

Sue: History for 400.

Albert: The year the Beatles invaded the United States.

Dr. T: (*smashing button, then struggling with his answer*) What is 1492?

Albert: What are you, an idiot? Sue?

Sue: What is 1964?

Albert: Right again, Sue. You've got a thousand now.

Sue: Geography for 100.

Albert: A country that borders the United States.

Sue: (*pushes button*) What is Canada?

Albert: Correct! Go again! (*The doctor is angry and frustrated; refuses to play*)

Sue: Geography for 200.

Albert: The country other than the U.S. that borders Canada.

Sue: What is Mexico?

Albert: Right again. Geography for 300? A big country with lots of people that's located near Pakistan.

Sue: What is Indiana?

Albert: Right again! For 400: The ocean right off of that country's coast.

Sue: What is...the Indiana Ocean?

Albert: Correct! Final category: Language.

Sue: 100 please, Albert.

Albert: The most common word in the English language.

Dr. T: (*wanting to play again*) What is the word *a*?

Albert: (*laughs*) Sue?

Sue: What is *awesome*?

Albert: Right again! Go for two! The number of times a day this word is used by the average person.

Sue: What is 1000?

Albert: Oh, I'm sorry. That's wrong. Doctor? (*silence*) The answer is "What is 1492?" Language for 300: When someone eats extra helpings of Tuesday's school lunch.

Dr. T: I suppose it's "What is awesome?"

Albert: Good try, Doctor. But that's wrong. Sue?

Sue: What is gastritis?

Albert: You got it! And now, our final Jeopardy answer: The 1980s phrase that gave rise to the most common word in our language.

Sue: That would be "What is totally awesome?"

Albert: Unbelievable! Once again, our champion moves on to tomorrow's round. (***Doctor T. storms off***) And thanks for playing "Teen Jeopardy"!

TEEN JEOPARDY GAMEBOARD

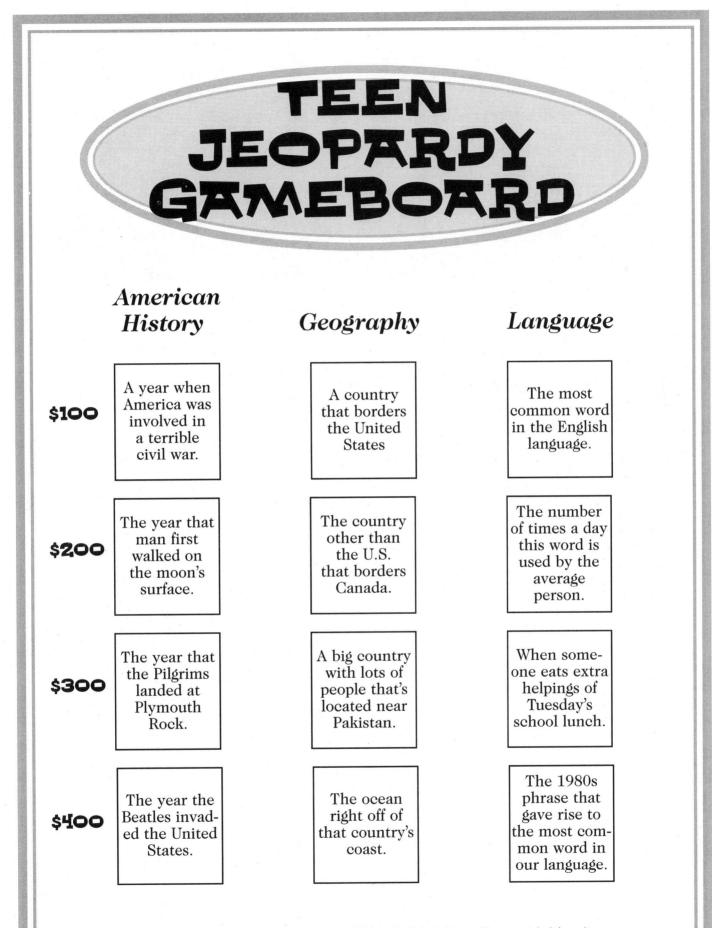

	American History	Geography	Language
$100	A year when America was involved in a terrible civil war.	A country that borders the United States	The most common word in the English language.
$200	The year that man first walked on the moon's surface.	The country other than the U.S. that borders Canada.	The number of times a day this word is used by the average person.
$300	The year that the Pilgrims landed at Plymouth Rock.	A big country with lots of people that's located near Pakistan.	When someone eats extra helpings of Tuesday's school lunch.
$400	The year the Beatles invaded the United States.	The ocean right off of that country's coast.	The 1980s phrase that gave rise to the most common word in our language.

TEEN JEOPARDY-THE GAME

After the sketch, it's time for everyone to play the game. Keep the same Albert as the host and use your version of the gameboard. Play the game by rotating the contestants after every question; that way more students can play. At the conclusion of the game, see if anybody stood out as a Jeopardy expert.

Small-group Discussion

Break up into groups of three and four. Have an adult with each group to lead the following discussion questions:

* Are there know-it-alls in your life?
* How do you treat them?
* In general, how are know-it-alls usually treated?

Now pass out Bibles and turn to the story of Joseph and his brothers in Genesis 37:3-8. Have someone read the story, then ask these questions:

* How would you feel if your brother or sister said what Joseph said to you?
* How many of you think you already *have* a brother or sister who acts like this?
* Do any of you ever feel like you're the one who is the know-it-all?
* If so, how do others treat you like a know-it-all?

Recap the rest of Joseph's story for your group briefly—how the brothers sold Joseph into slavery, but later Joseph rose to the top of the ranks in Egypt, as his dream had predicted. Sometimes the know-it-alls do know it all!

Then ask, "Is it hard to accept it when know-it-alls are right? Why?"

Story Time

Gather the group around for a short story time. Get a rocking chair, a small lamp, and turn the lights down. Read *Horton Hears a Who* by Dr. Seuss.

Conclusion

Remembering Horton and Joseph

When the story has finished, wrap it up:

Say to your group: Even though know-it-alls are frustrating and irritating, sometimes they're right—and the only appropriate response is to stop treating them poorly, and do something about ourselves. After all, we're the only people we can ever change. Everyone who mistreated Horton could have treated him better and changed the way they acted toward him. Joseph's brothers could have done the same—instead of mistreating their brother, they could have spent a little time focusing on the changes they needed to make.

Can we do the same? The only know-it-all you can change is yourself.

Close in prayer.

Loneliness

Every kid experiences loneliness—it's a part of life. It can also be very puzzling, especially when a kid feels lonely while surrounded by other people. If we want to sort out those mixed emotions and come to grips with our lonely feelings, we need to look at our Lord and his experiences with loneliness. This meeting is fairly serious and includes a gospel moment—a look at Jesus' work on the Cross and the response it demands from us.

Big Idea

Loneliness is part of the human condition—even Jesus felt loneliness—but God is with us, even during our loneliest times.

Key Text · Psalm 22:1-8, 14-24

¹My God, my God, why have you
   forsaken me?
   Why are you so far from saving me, so
   far from the words of my
   groaning?
²O my God, I cry out by day, but you do
   not answer,
   by night, and am not silent.
³Yet you are enthroned as the Holy One;
   you are the praise of Israel.
⁴In you our fathers put their trust;
   they trusted and you delivered them.
⁵They cried to you and were saved; in you
   they trusted and were not
   disappointed.
⁶But I am a worm and not a man,
   scorned by men and despised by
   the people.

⁷All who see me mock me;
   they hurl insults, shaking their
   heads:
⁸"He trusts in the Lord;
   let the Lord rescue him.
Let him deliver him,
   since he delights in him.

¹⁴I am poured out like water,
   and all my bones are out of joint.
My heart has turned to wax;
   it has melted away within me.
¹⁵My strength is dried up like a
       potsherd,
   and my tongue sticks to the roof of
   my mouth;
   you lay me in the dust of death.
¹⁶Dogs have surrounded me;
   a band of evil men has encircled
   me,

they have pierced my hands and
    my feet.
[17]I can count all my bones;
    people stare and gloat over me.
[18]They divide my garments among them
    and cast lots for my clothing.
[19]But you, O Lord, be not far off;
    O my Strength, come quickly to
    help me.
[20]Deliver my life from the sword,
    my precious life from the power of
    the dogs.
[21]Rescue me from the mouth of the
    lions;
    save me from the horns of the wild
    oxen.

[22]I will declare your name to my
    brothers;
    in the congregation I will praise
    you.
[23]You who fear the Lord, praise him!
    All you descendants of Jacob,
    honor him!
    Revere him, all you descendants of
    Israel!
[24]For he has not despised or disdained
    the suffering of the afflicted one;
he has not hidden his face from him
    but has listened to his cry for help.

What You'll Need for This Session

❋ Cassette tape of classic "lonely" songs you've taped, such as "Only the
    Lonely" by Roy Orbison (see **Before the Meeting**, point 1)
❋ TV, VCR, *The Lion King* video (see **Before the Meeting**, point 2)
❋ Sheets of paper, pencils, and a dictionary (see **Cell Groups**, page 120)
❋ Stick or yardstick (see **Before the Meeting**, point 4)
❋ Reminders to use in **Final Blessing** (page 121) such as small crosses, costume
    jewelry, or other simple objects

And if you want to do the options...

❋ *Jesus* video and the *Edge TV* (Vol. 4) segment "Loneliness" (see **Before the
    Meeting**, point 5)

Before the Meeting

1. As kids are coming in, have your tape of classic "lonely" songs playing in the
background.

2. Cue *The Lion King* to the scene where the young lion has left his homeland
and entered the jungle (see **Video Clip**, page 120).

3. Ask three adults to share, with the group, personal examples of lonely times
(see **Lonely Talks**, page 121).

4. Ask two students, in advance, for their help in the **Scripture Safari** section of

this program. One will read a Scripture passage while the other portrays a lonely Jesus (see **Scripture Safari**, page 121).

And if you want to do the options...

5. Cue the *Jesus* video to the scene at the Garden of Gethsemene, and the *Edge TV* video to the "Feature Story: Loneliness" (see **More Video Clips**, page 120).

Introduction

Lonely Hearts Club

Fade out your tape of classic "lonely" songs and welcome everybody to the meeting. Tell your group that today's topic is loneliness and, of course, nothing expresses loneliness quite like great country western music. Read the following list of country song titles, and have them vote on which one they think is best.

❋ "The Last Word in Lonesome Is Me"
❋ "Home Is Where the Hurt Is"
❋ "I Got Tears in My Ears from Lying on My Back Crying the Blues over You"
❋ "It Only Rains on Me"
❋ "Thank God and Greyhound She's Gone"
❋ "She Sure Makes Leavin' Look Easy"
❋ "Somebody Shoot out the Jukebox"
❋ "You Done Stomped on My Heart, and You Mashed That Sucker Flat"
❋ "What's a Fool Like Me Doin' in a Love Like This"

After you've read the list and the group has voted, introduce the following game.

SARDINES

This is a classic adaptation of Hide and Seek. You need a few rooms to play it in. (You people with those century-old churches and no gym may not know that you have the perfect Sardines facility.) Ideally, use your whole facility with the lights out, and this one rule: No one can open any doors that are closed.

To start the game, gather the whole group together and choose one person to go and hide. After two minutes, let everyone else go looking for this person. When people find the hidden person, they join him or her in the same hiding place. Eventually, more and more kids will find the growing sardine group until there's only one person who has not found the bunch. This person hides first for the next round. Allow plenty of time to play Sardines—it takes a while to complete each round.

When the game is over, sit everyone down and ask the people who were the last ones to find the group's hiding place how it felt. Was it a little creepy when they realized they were the only ones left? Did they want to find everyone just to eliminate the silence? Was it a lonely feeling?

Video Clip

After the questions—

Say to your group: *The feeling of being alone is something we all experience sometimes, even when there are people all around us. It's called loneliness, and it's one of the most painful things we ever experience. Let's watch this scene from the video,* The Lion King.

Cell Groups

After you've shown the video clip, break everybody up into groups of three to five students each, with an adult leading each group. Give each group a sheet of paper and a pencil.

Say to your group:

※ *Describe a lonely time in your life. What made you feel so lonely?*

※ *Does loneliness only happen when you're by yourself? Who can remember feeling lonely even when there were lots of people around?*

See if the groups can come up with a one-sentence definition of the word *lonely* and have them write it out.

After 10 minutes, bring everybody back together. Have a person from each group read their definition. Then read the definition of *lonely* from the dictionary.

Option

MORE VIDEO CLIPS

Show the "Loneliness" segment from *Edge TV* (Vol. 4). This is a great discussion starter to get kids thinking seriously about the subject.

Ask, "Do you think Jesus Christ ever felt this way? Let's watch this clip from the movie *Jesus.*" Show the clip.

When the scene concludes, break into your small groups again to discuss the following:

※ Why was Jesus lonely here? What circumstances caused him to feel this way?

※ Have you ever felt the same way? Why or why not?

※ Have your friends ever done the same thing to you?

※ Have you ever been overwhelmed with a problem that the people around you—family or friends—just didn't seem to understand? What was the situation? How did you handle it?

Lonely Talks

Have the three adults you asked ahead of time, tell the group about one of the loneliest times of their lives. Give each adult three or four minutes to share what happened and how he or she worked through it.

Scripture Safari

When they've finished, introduce Psalm 22:1-8, 14-24. Then—

Say to your group: Jesus had some lonely times, but none lonelier than hanging on the cross. He even felt like God had forsaken him. It was incredibly lonely, but even in the midst of that, God was still there helping him go through an unbelievably difficult time. Let's listen to the passage.

Turn the lights down low and have the student you chose in advance, walk slowly through the group with a stick, stand at the front of the group, and then drape his or her arms around the stick as if he or she is hanging on the cross. Have the second student read from Psalm 22 as the first student remains "on the cross."

When the reading is done, pray the following prayer:

Lord, we know that you felt lonely and forsaken as you hung on the cross in a way we can never fully understand. We, too, feel lonely sometimes, God, and wonder why no one seems to care. Help us, Lord, to realize that you're never far from us, that you understand what our loneliness is like, and that you're always willing to walk beside us when we feel isolated from everyone else. Thanks, God, for being with us in lonely times. In Jesus' name we pray. Amen.

Conclusion

Final Blessing

Say to your group: There's no way to simply erase our lonely feelings. But it does help to know that when we feel incredibly alone, God is right there with us. He's promised to never leave us or forsake us—ever! When you're feeling really lonely, don't forget that Jesus knows what it's like, and he'll be there.

Close with a blessing by reading Numbers 6:24-26. Explain to the kids what a blessing is: a reminder of God's presence and care for them. (Your group may be familiar with a blessing that's given at the end of a worship service.) This blessing is powerful—a reminder that God's presence is with them as they leave. Have them look at you as you read the passage.

To "seal" the blessing symbolically, give each student a small reminder of Christ as they leave. This could be a small cross, a piece of costume jewelry, a key, or anything simple that they may carry with them during the week. Ask them to bring their reminders back next week. When they do, have kids share about lonely moments they experienced during the week, and how they got through it knowing God was there with them.

Mouth (and what's inside it)

Inside your mouth is a very interesting muscle. It's a weird looking thing, isn't it? For such an odd piece of work, it's a powerful item. When under control, the tongue can create wonderful beauty; but out of control, it can be as deadly as a venomous snake. Gossip, swearing, anger, lying—they're all results of the uncontrolled tongue. God urges us to control our mouths and use our tongues for his glory rather than destruction.

Big Idea

Our mouths must be controlled or they'll cause a lot of damage.

Key Text · James 3:3-12

³When we put bits into the mouths of horses to make them obey us, we can turn the whole animal. ⁴Or take ships as an example. Although they are so large and are driven by strong winds, they are steered by a very small rudder wherever the pilot wants to go. ⁵Likewise the tongue is a small part of the body, but it makes great boasts. Consider what a great forest is set on fire by a small spark. ⁶The tongue also is a fire, a world of evil among the parts of the body. It corrupts the whole person, sets the whole course of his life on fire, and is itself set on fire by hell.

⁷All kinds of animals, birds, reptiles and creatures of the sea are being tamed and have been tamed by man, ⁸but no man can tame the tongue. It is a restless evil, full of deadly poison.

⁹With the tongue we praise our Lord and Father, and with it we curse men, who have been made in God's likeness. ¹⁰Out of the same mouth come praise and cursing. My brothers, this should not be. ¹¹Can both fresh water and salt water flow from the same spring? ¹²My brothers, can a fig tree bear olives, or a grapevine bear figs? Neither can a salt spring produce fresh water.

What You'll Need for This Session

❋ Beef tongue (available at most grocery stores and butcher shops) in a paper bag (see **Tongue Talk**, pages 125-126)
❋ Tape or CD of the Wayne Watson song "Sticks and Stones" on his *Home Free* album (see **Scripture Safari**, page 127), a tape deck or CD player.
❋ Whiteboard or newsprint and markers (see **Anger**, page 128)
❋ Two copies of the sketch **Oh, God** (pages 130-131)
❋ Posterboard and pens (see **Group Charter**, page 129)

And if you want to do the options...

❋ Stopwatch or clock with a second hand (see **Armless Charades**, page 125)
❋ Newsprint and scissors (see **Tongue Talk**, pages 125-126)
❋ Cardboard box, X-acto knife, markers, old socks, and breath mints (see **Before the Meeting** below, point 3)
❋ Food items (including hot dogs) and a blindfold (see **Taste Test**, page 126)
❋ Soda crackers, peanut butter, and a butter knife (see **Sticky Tongue**, page 126)
❋ Plastic trash can and a Nerf basketball (see **MJ Jam**, page 126)
❋ Ruler and candy waxed lips (see **Measure the Mouth**, page 127)
❋ TV, VCR, self-produced video, and the oldies tune, "You Talk Too Much" (see **Before the Meeting** below, point 4)

Before the Meeting

1. Select two females to perform the sketch **Oh, God** (see **Swearing**, page 128).

And if you want to do the options...

2. If **Foot in Your Mouth** (page 126) is one of the games you choose to play, you'll need to draw the face of a man on the side of a cardboard box. Cut out a large hole for the mouth.

3. During the week before your meeting, videotape all sorts of people sticking out their tongues (or opening their mouths very wide). Find a recording of the oldies tune "You Talk Too Much" (see **Video Clip**, page 127).

Introduction

Armless Charades

Begin the meeting with a game of charades—though with a twist.

Say to your group: This game of charades is different than traditional Charades. You won't guess movie, book, or song titles. Nor can you use hand signals to show the number of words and syllables. You'll communicate only with facial expressions and body language.

Invite people to come up and communicate a phrase while the rest of the group guesses. You can play just for fun or create two teams for a little competition. Time contestants and keep a running total for each team. The team with the lowest overall time wins. Some phrases you can use:

❋ I lost my dog.
❋ I'm angry at my parents.
❋ I got an F on my report card.
❋ I just bought a new CD.
❋ I haven't brushed my teeth today.
❋ I'm afraid of flying.
❋ I want an ice cream cone.
❋ I think I just saw Elvis.
❋ I get picked on at school.
❋ I'm running for president.
❋ I'm in love with a Coke machine.
❋ I forgot to do my homework.
❋ I'm looking for Santa Claus.
❋ I'm moving next week.
❋ I have to get glasses.
❋ I have a baby-sitting job.
❋ I have a monster in my closet.
❋ I'm really 30 years old.
❋ I'd rather not be doing this.
❋ I'm new in this group.

Option

If you have any announcements to make, try acting them out without using words.

Tongue Talk

When you've finished playing charades—

Say to your group: *It's tough to communicate without words, isn't it? That's why God gave us our mouths and that amazing muscle, the tongue.*

Now take the beef tongue out of its bag and show it to the group. Flap it around, point out its taste buds, and pretend to carry on a conversation with it. If you want to be really goofy, draw a cow face on newsprint and have two people hold it up. Cut a hole at the mouth, have someone hang the tongue through it from the back, and fake a conversation with the cow. (I said it was goofy.)
Still holding the tongue—

Say to your group: *Today we will discover some of the trouble this thing can cause us. But first, let's have a little more fun!*

Following are four off-the-wall games to play, each with a tongue theme. Select what's best for your needs.

FOOT IN YOUR MOUTH

Set up your cardboard box man and have everyone in the group take a shot at throwing a wadded up sock at the mouth from a distance. Give a breath mint (get it?) to each person who throws the sock in the mouth.

TASTE TEST

Place a couple of food items on a table. Blindfold volunteers who will taste each item and guess what it is. Make sure the last item they taste is a piece of hot dog. Have volunteers take off their blindfolds to see what they tasted. Before they remove their blindfolds, replace the hot dog with the beef tongue (off of which you've cut a piece), and let the kids think they actually tasted a piece of it.

STICKY TONGUE

Feed a few volunteers soda crackers with peanut butter on them until the volunteers' mouths are pretty full. The first one to successfully say "The rain in Spain falls mainly on the plain" wins.

MJ JAM

Basketball star Michael Jordan is famous for sticking his tongue out when he makes one of his amazing slam dunks. Put a large garbage can in the middle of the floor and have volunteers slam dunk—with their tongues hanging out, of course. Rate the dunks on a scale from 1-10.

MEASURE THE MOUTH

Use a ruler to measure the mouths of everyone in the group. Award candy waxed lips to whoever has the largest mouth.

Option

VIDEO CLIP
Play your self-produced tongue video to the oldies
tune "You Talk Too Much."

Scripture Safari

When you're done with your games—

Say to your group: *We've had a lot of fun with the tongue. But in all seriousness, the tongue is one of the most powerful things in the world. It has created and destroyed nations, enhanced and broken personalities, encouraged and devastated lives. Used correctly, it can build up; used incorrectly, it can tear down. The Bible even refers to its power.*

Read James 3:3-12 aloud. Then play the song "Sticks and Stones" from Wayne Watson's *Home Free* album (Day Spring). It offers a fresh focus on the James passage.
When the song has finished—

Ask your group:
✳ *Why is it so difficult to control our tongues?*
✳ *How is the tongue like a small fire?*
✳ *What is the problem of "fresh water from an unclean well"?*

Say to your group: *Our tongues can cause us problems if they are not used correctly. Let's look at four ways an uncontrolled tongue can hurt us.*

Gossip

Divide the group into equal smaller groups, (if you have a small youth group, staying together is fine). Have one person from each group come to you and, without the others hearing, tell her a phrase (i.e., "I am moving to Los Angeles because I like the weather"). Have each person go back to her group and whisper (without others hearing) the phrase to the person on her left. That person passes on the phrase to the next person, and so on. When the phrase is whispered to the last person in the group, have him repeat the phrase aloud. It probably will be quite different from the original phrase.
Then—

Say to your group: *We can see how easy it is for innocent facts to get garbled. That's what makes gossip such a killer. Let's get gossip under control by practicing these two principles:*

✳ *If you have a problem with someone, go directly to that person first and to no one else.*

❋ *If someone wants to talk to you about someone else, cut them off immediately. Challenge them to go directly to that person with the issue.*

When we put these two principles into practice, we'll do amazing things for God's kingdom. We'll also feel more secure because we know that others won't talk behind our backs either.

Anger

Read Proverbs 29:11. "A fool gives full vent to his anger, but a wise man keeps himself under control."

Ask your group:
❋ *When is anger justified?*
❋ *When is anger wrong?*

Next, have your group brainstorm practical ways to deal constructively with anger. Write their ideas out on a whiteboard or newsprint.

Now ask for two volunteers to come forward and role play an argument with each other. Explain that when you tell them to hold their tempers, the argument continues but now they must hold their tongues with their fingers. The results are pretty funny.

Swearing

Have your preselected volunteers come forward and perform the sketch, **Oh, God**.

When the sketch has finished—

Say to your group: *James 3:9-10 points out the inconsistency of praise and cursing coming out of the same mouth. James says, "My brothers, this should not be." Swearing, cussing, or cursing does not honor God. Let's work to be good examples of who God is and what he represents.*

Ask your group:
❋ *How is swearing a bad example?*
❋ *What can we do to keep from swearing?*

Offer examples of other phrases that aren't vulgar that could be used in times of frustration or pressure.

Lying

Say to your group: *Lying gives us a false sense of control or power. We may feel we have managed a situation successfully, but that's not true. Lying is like microwave popcorn. The little kernels sit peaceably in their package. But when the microwave heats them up, the package grows bigger and bigger. When the heat of daily living is on, we sometimes lie. But like the package* *of popcorn, the lies grow and grow until finally they get out of hand*

This analogy is from *More Junior High TalkSheets* by David Lynn (Youth Specialties/Zondervan, 1992).

Read to your group this dilemma:

Christy borrowed a sweater from Danielle. Danielle tells Christy that she needs the sweater returned. Christy had spilled juice on the sweater and made a small stain on the sleeve. She's considering her options: return the sweater and pretend nothing happened; avoid Danielle until she calls and asks for it again; tell Danielle that her dog wrecked the sweater; or tell the truth.

Ask your group:

❋ *What are the advantages and disadvantages of each option?*
❋ *What would you do? Why?*
❋ *What should you do? Why?*

Tongues under Control

Spend a few minutes covering these hints on how to create a strategy to keep our tongues under control:

❋ *Commit to using your tongue for good.* The first step in dealing with any life issue is to make a decision on what you're going to do. Let's choose the high road.

❋ *Ask God for help.* He has the power to enable you to win in this area.

❋ *Consider the consequences.* What are the consequences if you lose control over your tongue? An honest answer can motivate you to control your tongue.

❋ *Have others hold you accountable.* Your friends can check up on you and help you keep your tongue in its proper place.

Conclusion

Group Charter

Draw up a group charter that declares that your group is committed to keeping the tongue in control. Have the entire group sign the charter. Post it in your meeting room. (You might also want to send a copy to your church elders.)

Oh, God!

Two women are seated at a tennis match. Their heads are moving back and forth together as they watch the ball swatted over the imaginary net. A player evidently misses a shot; both women stop moving their heads, and Cindy speaks.

Cindy: Oh God, he missed the same shot twice in a row.

Laura: Oh, you talk to him, too?

Cindy: Huh? I wasn't talking to the player.

Laura: Not the player. <u>God</u>. Didn't I hear you just talk to him?

Cindy: Are you crazy? I don't even know the guy.

Laura: You just said, "Oh God."

Cindy: That's just an expression. Be quiet and watch the match. ***(heads move again, then stop abruptly)***

Laura: ***(with same intonation as Cindy said "Oh God")*** Oh Susie, he should have had that.

Cindy: What? Who are you talking to?

Laura: Nobody, it's just an expression.

Cindy: What's the matter with you?

Laura: If you use God's name to emphasize your disappointment with a missed shot, can't I use someone else's name? In fact, I'll use your name next time.

Cindy: You can't do that!

Laura: Why not?

Cindy: Because...because it's just plain stupid—that's why.

Laura: ***(pointing to the match)*** Here's the serve. ***(heads move, then stop)*** Oh, Cindish darn it! Did you see that?

Cindy: What'd you say?

Laura: Cindish darn it. You know, like gosh darn it. Only I changed the name.

Cindy: But you can't use my name.

Laura: Why not? You use God's name.

Cindy: That's different!

Laura: What do you mean? You don't even know him and you use his name as an "expression." But I use your name and you get upset.

Cindy: This is ridiculous. If I had known you were such a religious fanatic, I wouldn't have asked you to come along.

Laura: Okay, okay. I'm sorry. It's just that I get tired of people using my God's name as a silly expression to swear by. What if I used your dad's name, or the name of someone you loved every time I wanted to vent my frustration? You'd think I was making fun of them. I love God and I don't like people being trivial or flippant with him or his name. Besides...if you keep calling his name, he just might answer back.

Cindy: I think I see what you're saying.

Laura: Hey, how about I go get us a couple Cokes?

Cindy: Sounds good! *(Laura leaves, and Cindy's head again follows the imaginary ball—then stops suddenly)* I can't believe it—he lost the set...oh, God...

Voice over PA: You called?